EAST ASIAN DYNAMISM

DILEMMAS IN WORLD POLITICS

Series Editor
George A. Lopez, University of Notre Dame

Dilemmas in World Politics offers teachers and students of international relations a series of quality books on critical issues, trends, and regions in international politics. Each text will examine a "real world" dilemma and will be structured to cover the historical, theoretical, practical, and projected dimensions of its subject.

EDITORIAL BOARD

BOOKS IN THIS SERIES

Steve Chan
**East Asian Dynamism: Growth, Order, and
Security in the Pacific Region**

☐   ☐   ☐

Deborah J. Gerner
**One Land, Two Peoples:
The Conflict over Palestine**

☐   ☐   ☐

Kenneth W. Grundy
**South Africa: Domestic Crisis
and Global Challenge**

☐   ☐   ☐

Janet Welsh Brown and Gareth Porter
World Politics and the Global Environment

☐   ☐   ☐

Leon Lindberg
Europe 1992

EAST ASIAN DYNAMISM

■ ■ ■

Growth, Order, and Security in the Pacific Region

Steve Chan
University of Colorado

Westview Press
BOULDER □ SAN FRANCISCO □ OXFORD

Dilemmas in World Politics Series

Internal design by Libby Barstow. Cover design by Polly Christensen.

Published in 1990 in the United States of America by Westview Press, Inc., 5500 Central Avenue, Boulder, Colorado 80301, and in the United Kingdom by Westview Press, Inc., 36 Lonsdale Road, Summertown, Oxford OX2 7EW

Library of Congress Cataloging-in-Publication Data
Chan, Steve.
  East Asian dynamism : growth, order, and security in the Pacific region / Steve Chan.
    p. cm.—(Dilemmas in world politics.)
  Includes bibliographical references and index.
  ISBN 0-8133-7931-8. ISBN 0-8133-7932-6 (pbk.)
    1. East Asia—Economic policy. 2. East Asia—Politics and government. 3. East Asia—Economic integration. I. Title. II. Series.
HC460.5.C4 1990
338.95—dc20   90-12418
                                                                                          CIP

Printed and bound in the United States of America

∞ The paper used in this publication meets the requirements
    of the American National Standard for Permanence of Paper
    for Printed Library Materials Z39.48-1984.

10   9   8   7   6   5   4   3   2   1

For Jennifer and Andrew

Contents

□   □   □

Tables and Figures

□ □ □

Preface and Acknowledgments

This book offers a succinct treatment of the political economy of the Pacific region for both advanced undergraduate students and beginning graduate students. It combines perspectives from such social science disciplines as sociology, economics, history, and political science. It offers some substantive explanations of the recent experiences of Pacific Rim countries (especially the East Asian ones) and suggests some possible scenarios for their future development.

The first book in Westview's Dilemmas in World Politics series and faithful to the thematic focus of the series, it emphasizes the concepts of *policy choice* and *policy dilemma*. The discussion of these concepts is organized around the three cardinal values of economic growth, socio-political stability, and military and resource security. Through the presentation of alternative theoretical perspectives and the illustration of country-specific materials, three main arguments are put forth: (1) there is a variety of competing policy practices (or strategies) for the achievement of these values (each with its own promises and liabilities); (2) there are important and often nonobvious trade-offs in the pursuit of these values; and (3) there are significant cross effects between domestic and foreign developments. These three arguments buttress the central themes of policy choice and dilemma.

I am grateful for the encouragement and support of various friends and colleagues during the preparation of this book. George Lopez, series editor for Westview's Dilemmas series, was responsible for getting me interested in this project. Jennifer Knerr, senior editor at Westview, was very supportive and helpful in moving the project along. Several members of the Dilemmas editorial board—Barry Hughes, Jeffry Frieden, Deborah Gerner, and Karen Mingst—gave useful suggestions in response to my initial book proposal. Harry Harding, Neil Richardson, Sheldon Simon, Donald Weatherbee, and Allen Whiting conscientiously reviewed the manuscript and provided extensive comments that helped to improve the final product. Marian Safran offered her expert editorial input, and Libby Barstow was instrumental in seeing the book through its final production stage. Finally, my wife, Jennifer, has been a constant source of support and understanding in this as in other projects.

Steve Chan

□ □ □

Acronyms

ASEAN	Association of Southeast Asian Nations
EEC	European Economic Community, or Common Market
GATT	General Agreement on Tariffs and Trade
GNP	gross national product
MITI	Ministry of International Trade and Industry
MNC	multinational corporation
NATO	North Atlantic Treaty Organization
NIC	newly industrializing country
OMA	orderly marketing agreement
PLA	People's Liberation Army
PRC	People's Republic of China
UN	United Nations
VER	voluntary export restraint

EAST ASIAN DYNAMISM

ONE

□ □ □

The Pacific Region at the End of the Twentieth Century

We live in a rapidly changing world. As we prepare to enter the twenty-first century, developments in both the Atlantic and the Pacific areas portend major changes in the structure of the international political economy and the balance of global strategic force. In 1992, the member countries of the European Economic Community will remove their trade and immigration barriers. Therefore, Western Europe is poised to become one vast economic market while continuing its process of social, cultural, and political integration. Combining the assets of countries such as West Germany, France, Britain, and Italy promises to give them an enhanced collective voice in world affairs—perhaps even to the point of constituting a third center of global power, in addition to the United States and the Soviet Union.

Momentous events are also occurring in Eastern Europe, where because of popular pressure for economic and political liberalization, the authoritarian Communist rulers of Czechoslovakia, Bulgaria, East Germany, Hungary, Poland, and Romania fell from power in rapid succession in the final months of 1989. Under the leadership of Mikhail Gorbachev, the Soviet Union initiated a series of reforms to restructure its economic and political system. These reforms, however, have been unable to dampen and might have actually contributed to the outbreak of ethnic strife and secession movements in this vast country. After four and one-half decades, the iron curtain separating the European Communist countries from the West is finally being lifted. Both the physical and

1

symbolic barriers between Eastern and Western Europe—as epitomized by the Berlin Wall—are being taken down.

In the Pacific region, equally momentous changes have been taking place. Japan now commands the third largest economy in the world (the Japanese gross national product ranks only behind those of the United States and the USSR). Although Tokyo's current military capability is relatively limited in comparison to its economic and technological prowess, this capability can easily be upgraded on short notice—thereby enabling Japan to become a potential balance tipper in the U.S.-Soviet rivalry. Moreover, the absence of a visible military outreach capacity is compensated by an energetic and well-endowed foreign assistance program: Japan has now overtaken the United States as the world's largest donor of foreign aid.

The Pacific region also features the rapid ascendance of several *newly industrializing countries* (NICs) in recent decades. Collectively known sometimes as the "gang of four" or the "four little tigers," South Korea, Taiwan, Hong Kong, and Singapore have been phenomenally successful in their export drives and in exploiting this export expansion as an engine for domestic growth. Together with Japan, these smaller Asian countries have been responsible for much of the U.S. trade deficit and have consequently been the main targets of U.S. protectionism. With their rapidly rising income level and industrial maturity, they are on the threshold of joining the ranks of developed countries.

The looming presence of the People's Republic of China (PRC) is a constant factor in the evolving Pacific region. Beijing commands an enormous population, a large territorial expanse, and a potentially lucrative market for foreign trade and investment. It also has a large standing army equipped with nuclear weapons. For all these reasons, the "China factor" has been prevalent in U.S. as well as Soviet strategic thinking. Of course, this China factor will assume even greater importance if Beijing is able to accelerate its program of economic modernization without endangering domestic political stability. Any realignment of Chinese foreign policy will surely arouse grave concern in Washington, Moscow, and Tokyo.

The Pacific region also includes, at its northern reaches, Soviet Siberia and western Canada, with their vast natural wealth in lumber, minerals, and agricultural resources. Similarly, we find other resource-rich countries—especially Indonesia and Australia—toward the southern end of this region. These economies have been increasingly drawn into a regional system of economic exchange, with Japan acting as a prominent exporter of capital, technology, and heavy industrial products and as a major importer of agricultural goods and industrial raw materials.

The United States, of course, is very much an active and important player in the Pacific regional system. Economic and demographic trends point to a continued westward shift, so that California—already the nation's most populous and productive state—will assume an even more dominant role. The economy of the West Coast will become particularly oriented toward and dependent on economic transactions with the Pacific Rim countries. However, these countries are important for the United States not just because of commercial considerations. The United States after all has fought its three most recent and devastating wars in the Pacific region (the Vietnam War, the Korean War, and World War II, which, for the United States, started as a result of the Japanese attack against Pearl Harbor). Therefore, this region evidently also commands crucial strategic importance for Washington.

THE SCOPE AND DIVERSITY
OF THE PACIFIC REGION

The policy importance of the Pacific region is buttressed by its sheer size and remarkable dynamism. At the same time, this size and dynamism imply considerable regional diversity and complexity, which make efforts to cope with the region's evolving problems a very challenging task.

Figure 1.1 illustrates this challenge. The map shows that the Pacific Basin encompasses an enormous area. On one side of this basin lies North America, where Canada and the United States are located. Further south, we find the countries of Central and South America (such as Mexico and Chile), areas that will, however, be outside the scope of this book. On the other side of the Pacific Basin, the East Asian mainland is principally occupied by the PRC. Korea (its northern as well as southern parts) and Japan are situated to the northeast of the PRC and are the most industrialized parts of Asia. Further to the north are Siberia and Sakhalin Island, both territories of the Soviet Union. To the south of the PRC is Indochina, consisting of the Communist states of Vietnam, Laos, and Cambodia (also known as Kampuchea). Forming a semicircular arc around these Indochinese countries are the members of the Association of Southeast Asian Nations (ASEAN) and Papua New Guinea. The ASEAN members are Thailand, Malaysia, Singapore, Brunei, Indonesia, and the Philippines. Oceania, consisting of Australia and New Zealand, is situated even further south. Finally, several island groups, such as Micronesia, Melanesia, Polynesia, and Hawaii, lie in the middle of the Pacific Ocean.

A variety of ethnic groups, cultural traditions, economic systems, and political ideologies exists around the Pacific Basin. The countries of North America and Oceania—namely, the United States, Canada, Australia,

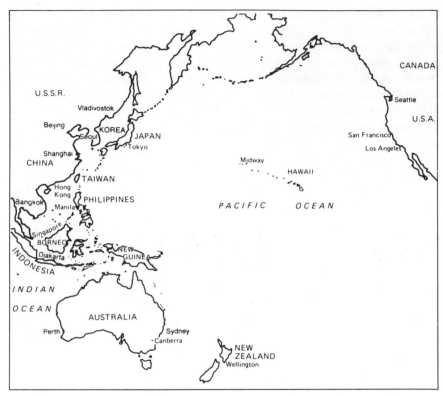

Figure 1.1 The Pacific region

and New Zealand—have a great deal in common. They are former British colonies, settled mainly by white immigrants from Europe. Consequently, they share a common language, religion, economic system, and political institutions inherited from the British. They are all English-speaking and predominantly Protestant countries, with a tradition of pluralistic politics and a developed capitalist economy.

The countries of East and Northeast Asia also tend to share a common cultural legacy—with its source in China. Japan, Korea, Taiwan, Hong Kong, and to some extent, Singapore have been deeply influenced by Confucianism. However, they are also marked by important economic and political differences. Japan is, of course, a highly industrialized society that has had democratic institutions since the end of World War II. Like Japan, South Korea, Taiwan, Singapore, and Hong Kong have capitalist economies based on the principles of market competition. They differ from the so-called command economies of the PRC and North Korea, where the government instead of the market assumes the primary role of determining the supply and the price of goods. Additionally, whereas each of the former countries has in recent years liberalized its political system to allow more personal freedom and electoral contest, political dissent is still not tolerated in the PRC or North Korea, as shown by the bloody suppression of the prodemocracy demonstrators in Beijing in June 1989.

The Southeast Asian countries are a rather heterogeneous group. This is understandable because they are geographically located at the intersection of Indian, Chinese, Middle Eastern, and Western cultural influences. Thus, for example, we find Islam (Indonesia and Malaysia), Buddhism (Thailand and Cambodia), and Catholicism (the Philippines) being practiced in different countries. As a result of earlier immigration, some countries such as Singapore and Malaysia also feature considerable ethnic diversity. In the Pacific region, the Southeast Asian countries (and the PRC) tend to have the lowest per capita income and the least economic development. This is especially true for the Indochinese Communist states, which face significant economic challenges. The Southeast Asian countries are also more vulnerable than other Pacific region countries to internal instability stemming from ethnic violence and political rebellion. Recent history further shows that they are prone to be drawn into rivalries among the great powers as pawns or as prizes.

THE IMPORTANCE
OF THE PACIFIC REGION

The map of the region (Figure 1.1) reveals why the great powers have drawn Pacific Rim countries into their rivalries. This region—especially Northeast Asia—is where the geographic reaches of the United States, the USSR, Japan, and the PRC come into contact. This proximity has brought about frequent conflicts of the political, economic, and military interests of these great powers. Thus, for example, in the past century, Japan was involved in wars against China and against Russia/the USSR. In World War II, moreover, it fought those adversaries plus the United States simultaneously. In the 1950s, when U.S. and Chinese soldiers clashed in Korea, Japan and the USSR were allied to opposite sides. And in the 1960s and early 1970s, the United States fought a losing war against North Vietnam, which was supported by the PRC and the Soviet Union. Finally, there are lingering border disputes between the PRC and the USSR, the USSR and Japan, and Japan and the PRC. In 1969, a military skirmish between the Chinese and Soviet border guards over a small island in the Ussuri River almost caused a war between these Communist giants.

More recently, there has been mounting economic friction between the capitalist countries on opposite sides of the Pacific Ocean. The East Asian trading nations have been very successful in penetrating the consumer markets of North America. These countries (e.g., Japan, Taiwan, South Korea) have compiled large surpluses in trading with the United States and have consequently aroused strong sentiments in favor of protectionism in the latter. The emerging division of economic labor in the Pacific Basin increasingly casts the United States and its English-speaking regional neighbors (Canada, Australia, New Zealand) in the role of suppliers of agricultural and mineral products (wheat, soybeans, beef, lumber, tobacco, petroleum, iron ore), and the East Asian market economies act as providers of manufactured goods. Thus, there have been important changes in the **terms of trade** (the balance of payments in foreign trade) as well as the **composition of trade** (the nature of the exports and imports: agricultural, mineral, manufactured, or industrial) in this region.

There is evidence for the view that the center of the global distribution of political, economic, and military power has moved from the Atlantic region to the Pacific region (see Table 1.1). The table displays data on the countries in the latter region (small countries such as Brunei, Fiji, and Nauru are omitted). By comparing the geographic area, population, gross national product, and military capability as reflected by defense expenditure one can see the relative size of the countries. Five of the world's largest territorial states are in this region (the USSR, Canada, the PRC, the United States, and Australia; Brazil, the world's fifth largest state, is excluded because it is in South America). Similarly, five of the seven most populous states border on the Pacific (the PRC, the USSR, the United States, Indonesia, and Japan). Indeed, the Pacific Rim countries account for 47.5 percent of the earth's land area and 44.7 percent of the earth's inhabitants.

The physical or demographic size of a country is not so important as its economic and military capability. The United States, the USSR, and Japan have the world's largest economies. The former two countries also possess the most powerful war machines in the world. In combination, the Pacific Rim countries are responsible for about 57.9 percent of global economic production and 67.2 percent of global military expenditures.

These aggregate statistics, however, are unable to suggest the dynamism of the Pacific region. Table 1.2 offers some comparative figures on the growth rate of gross domestic product during 1980–1986. It shows that the Pacific Rim economies have expanded much faster than their counterparts elsewhere. For the group of advanced market economies, the European average was 1.8 percent per year, whereas the Pacific average was 3.1 percent annually. In the upper-middle-income group, the per-

Table 1.1
Relative Size (Area, Population, Economy, Defense) of Pacific Rim Countries

	Area[1]	Population[2]	Economy[3]	Defense[4]
Northeast Asia				
Japan	144.0	122.0	2,369,000	24,320
South Korea	38.0	42.2	118,000	5,626
North Korea	47.0	21.4	25,900	5,800
East Asia				
PRC	3,692.0	1,074.0	470,700	20,660
Taiwan	14.0	19.8	101,300	4,701
Hong Kong	0.4	5.4	—	—
Southeast Asia				
Indonesia	735.0	180.4	65,780	1,367
Malaysia	128.0	16.1	28,970	937
Papua New Guinea	184.0	3.6	2,759	40
Philippines	116.0	61.5	34,620	458
Singapore	0.2	2.6	20,550	1,041
Thailand	198.0	53.0	45,070	1,657
Indochina				
Vietnam	128.0	63.6	12,700	2,479
Cambodia	70.0	6.5	—	—
Laos	70.0	3.8	573	58
Oceania				
Australia	2,968.0	16.1	197,900	4,986
New Zealand	104.0	3.3	33,910	755
North America				
United States	3,615.0	243.8	4,527,000	296,200
Canada	3,852.0	25.9	402,100	8,835
USSR	8,650.0	284.0	2,460,000	303,000
Pacific region as % of global total	47.5	44.7	57.9	67.2

[1]Area is measured in thousands of square miles.
[2]Population is measured in millions for 1987.
[3]Economy (gross domestic product) is measured in millions of U.S. dollars. The figures for Cambodia and Laos are for 1984, whereas figures for all other countries are for 1987.
[4]Defense is measured by military expenditures in 1987 (in millions of U.S. dollars). The figures for Papua New Guinea, Singapore, and Vietnam are for 1986, and that for Laos is for 1985.
Sources: U.S. Arms Control and Disarmament Agency, World Military Expenditures and Arms Transfers: 1988 (Washington, D.C.: author, 1989); and Hammond, Inc., World Atlas (New York: author, 1978).

formance of the Pacific Rim countries has been even more impressive. While their Latin American peers grew at a sluggish average pace of 0.2 percent annually, the Asian NICs had an average yearly gain of 6.2 percent. Except for the Philippines, which suffered an economic contraction during 1980–1986 (this is probably also true for the Indochinese states, but the pertinent data for them are unavailable), even the poorer

Table 1.2
Comparative Economic Performance: Average Annual Rate of Change
in Gross Domestic Product, 1980–1986

		Industrial Market Economies	
European		Pacific Rim	
Spain	1.8	New Zealand	2.6
Ireland	0.7	Australia	3.1
Italy	1.3	Japan	3.7
United Kingdom	2.3	Canada	2.9
Belgium	0.9	United States	3.1
Austria	1.8		
Netherlands	1.0		
France	1.3		
West Germany	1.5		
Finland	2.7		
Denmark	2.8		
Sweden	2.0		
Norway	3.5		
Switzerland	1.5		
Average	1.8	Average	3.1
		Upper-Middle-Income Countries	
Latin American		Pacific Rim	
Brazil	2.7	Malaysia	4.8
Mexico	0.4	South Korea	8.2
Uruguay	−2.6	Hong Kong	6.0
Panama	2.6	Singapore	5.3
Argentina	−0.8	Taiwan	6.8
Venezuela	−0.9		
Average	0.2	Average	6.2
		Lower-Middle-Income Countries	
Latin American		Pacific Rim	
Bolivia	−3.0	Indonesia	3.4
Dominican Republic	1.1	Philippines	−1.0
Honduras	0.6	Papua New Guinea	1.8
Nicaragua	0.2	Thailand	4.8
El Salvador	−1.0		
Guatemala	−1.2		
Paraguay	1.1		
Peru	−0.4		
Ecuador	1.8		
Colombia	2.4		
Average	1.6	Average	2.3
		Lower-Income Countries	
South Asian		Pacific Rim	
Bangladesh	3.7	PRC	10.5
India	4.9		
Pakistan	6.7		
Average	5.1		

Sources: World Bank, *World Development Report 1988* (New York: Oxford University Press, 1988), pp. 224–225; and Council for Economic Planning and Development, *Taiwan Statistical Data Book* (Taipei: author, 1987), p. 23.

Pacific Rim countries (Indonesia, Thailand, and especially the PRC) were able to achieve much faster growth rates than were their counterparts in Latin America or South Asia. In short, the recent superior economic performance of the Pacific region suggests that it is likely to make further gains relative to other areas of the world. Thus, the importance of the Pacific region in world affairs is likely to grow in coming years.

POLICY CHALLENGES TO GROWTH, ORDER, AND SECURITY

The rise of the Pacific region in world affairs poses policy challenges to those inside as well as outside the area. How can national governments successfully promote economic development or, in the case of the already developed countries such as the United States, industrial revitalization in an increasingly competitive environment? What are the most effective strategies for stimulating rapid economic growth, and is this rapid growth incompatible with the maintenance of political order and stability (both domestically and internationally)? And to the extent that differential economic growth rates imply upward or downward mobility for individual countries in the international system, what implications does this mobility have for the pursuit of national security and the preservation of regional peace?

The following chapters will address the cardinal policy values of *economic growth, political order,* and *military security.* The discussion will address in particular the policy challenges stemming from the pursuit of these values at both national and regional levels. The thematic focus will be on alternative perspectives on how these values can be most effectively achieved and on the trade-offs or incompatibilities sometimes posed by these values. There will not be any simple solution or magic formula for explaining or prescribing the management of growth, order, and security in the Pacific region. Instead, the accent will be on the *policy dilemmas* suggested by a complex and evolving reality. Indeed, for many of the topics to be discussed in the subsequent chapters, major differences of opinion exist among the relevant scholarly and policy communities.

THE BOOK'S PURPOSE AND ARCHITECTURE

Naturally, it would be impossible to compress a discussion of the entire complex and evolving reality of the Pacific region into a short book. As a result, I have been selective. Some countries and topics are deemphasized and even bypassed in favor of others. My intent is not to offer a text on physical or cultural geography. Nor do I intend to provide country-specific accounts as if writing a tour guide. Rather, I hope to apply certain contemporary social science perspectives and concepts to the Pacific reality in order to illuminate some salient policy problems and empirical patterns suggested by this reality. A conscientious effort is made to balance historical description with analytic explanation. I try in this book not only to account for the past but also to look into the future.

The book's organization is straightforward. Chapter 2 gives a brief history of the Pacific region, especially developments concerning the two East Asian giants, China and Japan. Chapter 3 outlines the policy dilemmas posed by the pursuit of economic growth, political order, and military security. It reviews the competing perspectives and practices pertaining to each member of this trinity of values and uses the experiences of individual Pacific Rim countries to highlight these differences. Chapter 4 focuses on the policy tension among the three values of growth, order, and security, and explains why it may be difficult to pursue them concurrently. Again, case materials are used to show the possible trade-offs among these values and to explore in particular the dilemmas posed to U.S. foreign policy conduct. Chapter 5 borrows several models of regional structure from the general literature of international political economy and, with a view to the future, tries to assess their applicability to the evolving Pacific region. The book concludes with discussion questions, a short list of recommended readings for students interested in deepening and extending further their understanding of the Pacific region, and a glossary of key concepts presented in this book.

TWO

□　□　□

East Meets West:
Historical Background

E ven as early as the time of the Roman Empire, there was regular commercial contact between Europe and China. Trade took place along the caravan routes winding through Central Asia. Although the journey was very hazardous because of the dangers posed by weather, terrain, and bandits, it was highly profitable. Chinese goods, especially silk and porcelain, were in great demand in Europe and fetched a handsome price. Indeed, so popular was Chinese silk as a fashion statement of the day that at one time the government of Rome had to ban it as a luxury item. Yet the wealthy Romans continued to wear silk—but they hid it under clothing made of coarser fabric. This might have been the origin of modern-day silk lingerie.

The riches and the grandeur of the fabulous East continued to fascinate Europeans of subsequent ages. This fascination was fueled by reports from travelers such as Marco Polo, who found a vast and wealthy Chinese empire. At the dawn of the modern era China was the world's largest territorial and most populous state, with the biggest economy. It also had the world's largest cities, where commerce and literature thrived.

By the fifteenth century, the rise of the Ottoman Empire in the Middle East increasingly threatened to cut off the traditional caravan routes connecting Europe to Asia. This pressure from the Muslims forced the Europeans to seek alternative ways to reach Asia. The impulse for exploration was most keenly felt by the Iberians. Christopher Columbus was able to convince the Spanish crown to provide him with a small fleet to look for a westerly sea route to China. His journey of 1492 gave him credit for discovering the New World. However, when he first came into contact with the American continent, he mistook it for India, which he believed to lie midway between Europe and China. As a consequence, the native people of America have been commonly called "Indians."

By the early sixteenth century, Europeans had successfully circumnavigated the globe and had set up provisioning stations and trading posts in different parts of the world. The Portuguese were first to establish a presence in Asia (Goa in India, Macao in China). They were followed by the Dutch (in Taiwan and Japan) and the Spaniards (in the Philippines). These early European traders and missionaries, however, were often rebuffed by the rulers of China and Japan and were usually restricted to a small enclave so that their contact with the native people could be more easily controlled.

Modest as these European enclaves were initially, they laid the groundwork for a global network of economic, cultural, and military outposts that was critical for the European domination of Asia in the subsequent centuries. In other words, whereas different parts of the world had previously existed in relative isolation from each other, now they were being integrated into one **world system** (whereby countries became tied to a global system of economic exchange). Peru, a Spanish colony, exported silver to Seville (in Spain) and Manila (in the Philippines, then a Spanish colony). In Seville, this silver was exchanged for Spanish primary goods (wine, wool) as well as North European manufactured goods. Similarly, in Manila, Spain exchanged exports from its American colonies for Asian goods (spice, silk, porcelain), which it in turn reexported to Europe. In this way, different continents were brought together in a single commercial and production system dominated by the Europeans. As we shall see, this emergent world system portended very significant changes for the prosperity and stability of the Pacific region.

Until the nineteenth century, however, the Asians were relatively successful in holding the European traders and missionaries at bay. The Chinese court assumed an aloof and patronizing attitude toward these Westerners, keeping them confined to the southern port cities of Macao and, later, Canton. China's rulers, supremely confident in their own tradition, professed little need for Western goods and ideas. Thus, responding to a British request for diplomatic representation in Beijing in 1816, the Chinese emperor avowed that "my dynasty attaches no value to products from abroad; your nation's cunningly wrought and strange wares do not appeal to me in the least, nor do they interest me."[1] Earlier, after hosting an audience for a Jesuit priest, a somewhat more sympathetic Chinese ruler had confided that the missionary had better give up his strange ideas about virgin birth and resurrection if he was to win any converts in the Celestial Empire.

This sense of self-confidence and, indeed, smugness stemmed from China's historical role in Asia. Unlike Europe, where several sovereign countries with relatively equal capabilities were constantly competing for power, China was a "world empire" without rivals in East Asia. It claimed suzerainty over its smaller neighbors, which had to pay tribute to the Chinese emperor as a sign of submission. The influence of Chinese political and cultural institutions was especially strong in Korea, Japan, and Annam (modern-day Vietnam). Thus, it is understandable why China assumed such a looming presence in the early modern history of the Pacific region.

To be sure, China was occasionally invaded by nomadic tribesmen from the north. These invasions brought about the rule by the Mongols and by the Manchus during the Yuan (1279–1368) and the Qing (1644–1911) dynasties respectively. However, despite these military setbacks, the Chinese felt secure in their sense of superiority, for their culture and society had always been able to absorb and assimilate alien forces. The Mongols and Manchus had to rely on Chinese bureaucracy and Confucian ideology to maintain their rule.

Confucianism, unlike Western religion, is a secular ideology, or code of ethics. It stresses the need for proper behavior of and harmonious relationships among various social actors (between the emperor and his subjects, father and son, husband and wife, and older and younger brothers). It values order, hierarchy, and tradition and assigns the central role of maintaining social control and regulation to the extended family. Because of this preeminent status given to the family, Confucianism promotes filial piety, ancestral worship, and collective responsibility.

The Chinese state and the dominant Confucian ideology managed to preserve social order and institutional continuity for more than two thousand years (from the establishment of the Han Dynasty in 206 B.C. to the Republican Revolution of 1911). The state and Confucianism were remarkably resilient. Yet, it was their past success in preserving order and continuity that made them ill equipped to cope with the Western assault in the nineteenth century.

CHINESE DECLINE
AND JAPANESE ASCENDANCE

Although the Chinese invented the concept of bureaucracy and had, as early as 206 B.C., created a system of open examination for recruiting meritorious officials, they failed to develop a strong state that was capable of meeting the Western challenge in the nineteenth century. And although at the beginning of the sixteenth century, China possessed an economy larger than those of the European countries and a technology at least as advanced as theirs, it lagged behind Europe in initiating capitalist industrialization. Finally, although China had a long coastline and many good ports, it did not send naval expeditions or trade missions abroad (except for a short period during the Ming Dynasty). In fact, during much of its history, emigration and foreign trade were banned by the imperial court.

In contrast, Britain, even though it was much smaller than China and far away from Asia, was able to establish a preeminent political and economic presence in the Pacific region by the middle of the nineteenth century. Britain also managed to colonize large areas, populating some of them (Australia, New Zealand, Canada, and the United States) with its own settlers and culture. And Japan, although commanding a much smaller resource and territorial base than China, was able to develop a strong state and to launch a successful industrialization program just when China was collapsing because of political disintegration and economic decay. How can we explain these puzzles?

Although China is a large country, only one quarter of its land is arable. Moreover, half of this arable land is dependent on irrigation in order to raise crops. This need for irrigation was in part responsible for the early development of a government bureaucracy, which undertook major water conservation and flood control projects. It also gave rise to an *intensive mode* of agricultural production, which emphasizes the use of *human labor* as a means of increasing crop yield, and is most evident in southern China where rice cultivation prevails. In contrast, the West, with its emphasis on grain and livestock, has traditionally practiced an *extensive mode* of agriculture (as exemplified by the American cowboys), which relies on *territorial expansion* rather than human labor as a means of increasing yield. Thus, China and the West undertook two very different forms of expansion. In the words of one observer, "China had in fact been expanding, but internally, extending its rice production within its frontiers."[2] Conversely, by the fifteenth century, European countries were exhausting the space needed for their extensive agronomy. The pressure to search for additional "living space" became one source of Western colonialism.

The European explorers were followed by settlers and colonial administrators, who claimed the foreign territories for their king and church. This colonial expansion soon assumed a momentum of its own, with diverse motivations like national glory, missionary zeal, commercial greed, and defense security. Thus, by the late nineteenth century, King Leopold of Belgium was able to declare, "The world has been pretty well pillaged already." With few exceptions (for example, China, Japan,

Thailand), European colonialism had encroached on the rest of the inhabited world. In the Pacific region, the chief British possessions included Hong Kong, Singapore, Malaya, New Zealand, Australia, and Canada. France had claimed Indochina, whereas the Netherlands had taken over Indonesia. Russia had pacified Central Asia, colonized Siberia, and appeared to have acquired a major influence in outer Mongolia and northern Manchuria. At the same time, U.S. territorial limits had reached beyond the West Coast. In 1898 the Hawaiian islands were annexed by Washington. In the same year, despite its avowed anticolonial heritage, the United States took over the Philippines as booty of the Spanish-American War. To many Americans, this westward expansion was a fulfillment of their country's "manifest destiny."

The attempt by the European countries to expand their frontiers both inside and outside Europe engendered *national rivalry*. This rivalry necessitated constant efforts to prepare for war and thus the organization of a powerful army and arms industry. The military, however, has always been a costly proposition. Thus, the European monarchs often had to raise money by borrowing from wealthy bankers and were compelled to develop a strong bureaucracy to extract taxes for military purposes. In its turn, the crown's military apparatus strengthened its bargaining position relative to that of the nobility. Thus, war financing and war fighting helped to create a tradition of strong states in Europe.[3]

Unlike the European system of rival powers, China was clearly the preeminent country in its "universe." Although China did undergo periods of fragmentation and disorder, it did not face the same kind of pressure for constant military preparation and the consequent stimulus to develop a strong state. There was a great deal of local autonomy in the enforcement of imperial edicts and the collection of taxes. In contrast to the European tradition of active monarchs who took a direct and personal role in deciding policies, the Chinese emperors customarily reigned rather than ruled.

Similarly, the competition among the European monarchs for mobile capital in order to strengthen their defense was relatively unknown in imperial China. Thus, according to one well-known scholar,[4] capitalist development conditioned upon war commissions and war loans did not take place there. The universal pacification of the Chinese empire, while conducive to the maintenance of order and stability, obviated one important stimulus for the development of European capitalism. Conversely, the frequent warfare and the armed peace among competing European powers had the effect of promoting strong states and capitalist development. Thus, we see an example of the sometimes paradoxical relationships among the values of economic growth, political order, and military security.

But why did Japan succeed where China had failed? The Meiji Restoration—a revolution from above, led by disgruntled members of the samurai (warrior) class—produced a strong state and rapid economic development. Unlike imperial China, traditional Japan was a feudal country. It was divided into many fiefs, each of them ruled by a feudal lord, a *daimyo*. The most powerful *daimyo* was Lord Tokugawa, whose administration, or shogunate, ruled in the name of the Japanese emperor. The Tokugawa shogun and his allies, however, controlled only 60 percent of the country's domains and thus had to guard constantly against disloyalty by the other *daimyo*. Consequently, the situation in Tokugawa Japan resembled more the armed rivalry of Europe than the imperial peace of China. Indeed, in 1868 the shugonate was overthrown by a rebellion led by two rival *daimyo*.

The Confucian orthodoxy that prevailed in both traditional China and Japan denigrated the merchant class. Upward social mobility was not possible for ordinary Japanese merchants. Moreover, the sale of land was outlawed in traditional Japan. The status of samurai was hereditary and for commoners, unless they were adopted, was beyond reach. Thus, Japanese merchants were forced to concentrate on business pursuits.[5] China's open social system, however, brought about completely different results. In imperial China, successful merchants could convert their wealth into social respectability: They could purchase land and thereby join the rural gentry class. They could also invest in their sons' education in the hope that the latter would successfully pass the imperial examination and become officials. Finally, they could buy official titles and literary degrees from the government. Instead of plowing their profits back to business ventures, Chinese merchant families sought to enter the officialdom and the rural rentier class. There was consequently a constant flight of talent and capital from business to economically less productive and socially more prestigious investments in titles, land, and classical education. The drain of business capital for status consumption was exacerbated by the fact that most Chinese titles could not be inherited. Therefore, if a son wanted to maintain the family's social standing, he had to repurchase his father's title. Thus, we encounter the paradox of a rigid and closed social structure (in Japan) helping to promote entrepreneurship and economic development and of a fluid and open social structure (in China) having the opposite effect.

Capitalist development was hampered in traditional China by the absence of primogeniture—the custom according to which the eldest son inherits all his father's property. Instead, in traditional China all sons were entitled to a share of their father's property. This practice, eminently fair according to contemporary standards, had several significant effects. One was the fragmentation of the family's financial resources.

Thus, Chinese peasants had very small and scattered plots, a situation hardly conducive to agricultural mechanization. Another effect was early marriages and large families. Inheritance shares provided the financial means for the male descendants to start their own families early. Thus, another indirect consequence was a severe population pressure in rural China and the concomitant tendency to pursue intensive agriculture with its emphasis on human labor. The explosion of the Chinese population in the nineteenth century was one cause of the declining standard of living and of the widespread social disorder and economic hardship that followed in its wake. Most important, the Chinese inheritance practice dissipated family wealth, so that even the richest families would have their wealth greatly diminished as a result of the successive divisions of the patrimony over several generations (especially because wealthy men often had several wives and were therefore especially likely to have a large number of heirs).

Unlike China but like England, traditional Japan practiced primogeniture. This custom tended to preserve family fortunes and promote capital accumulation essential for economic modernization. It pushed the younger sons to undertake social and economic pursuits unconnected with their fathers' occupation (in England, they usually joined the clergy, the military, or the colonial service). What is more, it delayed marriages and tempered population growth because, deprived of a share of the family inheritance, the younger sons had to establish an independent financial basis before considering marriage (especially if the bride's family demanded dowry as a condition for marriage). Thus, the existence of primogeniture facilitated social and economic modernization in Japan, and its absence in China had the reverse effect.

I mentioned earlier that the Chinese imperial system and the Confucian ideology, which had preserved social order and political stability over two thousand years, failed to meet the nineteenth-century challenge from the West. It gave Chinese officials an unwarranted sense of self-confidence and self-satisfaction. Moreover, because the Chinese elite—the officials, the gentry, and the literati—was closely identified with and legitimized by the Confucian ideology, its members were understandably loath to abandon this orthodoxy in exchange for Western values and ideas. In fact, the gentry-landlord class in China continued to be a strong reactionary force opposing land reform until the Communists broke its influence after 1949. The Japanese leaders, however, were not saddled with illusions about Confucianism or reluctance to adopt foreign ways. Having imported different aspects of the traditional Chinese culture at earlier times, they were ready and eager to learn from the West. Unlike the Chinese elite that still tried to maintain or salvage the old order, the samurai were ready to overthrow it. The rising inflation rate during the latter part of the Tokugawa era impoverished them—samurai were recipients of fixed stipends—thus reducing their allegiance to and support for the ancien régime. And having been detached from land possession at an earlier time, the samurai no longer presented a possible source of rural conservatism.

WESTERN IMPERIALISM
AND ASIAN NATIONALISM

The different developmental experiences of Japan and China cannot be entirely accounted for by their domestic factors. Their relations with the external world need to be included in order to provide a fuller explanation. As we have seen, a global system of economic production and exchange was formulated in the sixteenth century. By the mid-nineteenth century, this system had become much more extensive and vigorous. Lured by the prospects of huge profits or mass converts, Westerners had been knocking ever more insistently on China's door. Luckily for Japan, Western attention had been deflected toward the bigger prizes of China and India. Japan was therefore afforded a critical breathing space to undertake its self-strengthening programs.

More specifically, it was China's misfortune that the British acquired a taste for tea. The popularity of this staple was such that the British Parliament passed an act requiring the East India Company to keep a year's stock in supply at all times. By the 1860s, the British were consuming annually almost five pounds of tea per person.[6] The import of tea and the poor market for British goods in China led to an unfavorable balance of trade for London, and thus the outflow of specie (that is, precious metal such as silver) to China.

Britain's predicament, however, did not last long because it soon discovered that it could make a handsome profit by exporting to China opium produced in the British possessions of Bengal and Madras. By 1828, opium was responsible for 90 percent of the value of all foreign goods imported by China. The flood of opium into the Chinese market reversed the trade balance; in fact, there began a tremendous exodus of silver from China to Britain as a result of the former's payment for this commodity.

The export of opium more than solved London's earlier problem of paying for Chinese tea. By establishing this triangular commercial relationship between India, China, and itself, Britain was able to create a lucrative source of revenue for its colonial government in India and to use China as a conduit to bring home the profits from India. In this exchange, the growers and consumers of opium (the Indians and the Chinese) were both exploited for the benefit of the British.

The outflow of silver from China to pay for the illicit opium imports undermined its economy. Traditional Chinese economy operated on bimetallic—that is, silver as well as copper—standards. Taxes and major transactions were denominated in silver, whereas wages and smaller transactions were paid in copper. The outflow of silver made that metal more expensive, meaning that more and more copper was needed in exchange for the same amount of silver. This development had the practical effect of doubling and even tripling the peasants' tax obligations and was a major cause of rural unrest.

In addition to the unfavorable economic and political consequences of opium imports, the imperial court in Beijing was concerned with the undesirable social effects of mass addiction to this drug. Accordingly, the court issued numerous edicts banning its import and consumption, seized and burned opium stocks, and executed drug smugglers and users. Yet these tactics did not succeed in ending the import of the drug. Incredible as it may sound today, the British insisted on their right to sell opium in China in the name of free trade. This led to the infamous Opium War (1839–1842) between the two countries, a war in which China was easily defeated.

China's defeat in the Opium War not only was a source of national humiliation but also led to the first of many unequal treaties forced on the country by foreign powers. The Treaty of Nanjing stipulated that China cede Hong Kong to the British. In addition, five Chinese ports (Shanghai, Ningbo, Canton, Xiamen, and Fouzhou) were to be opened to foreign trade. The Chinese government could not regulate this trade, nor could it impose its own tariffs. Furthermore, it would not have any authority over British subjects residing in the foreign "concessions" on Chinese soil. This concept of *extraterritoriality* meant that foreign rather than Chinese laws would apply to foreigners living in China. In short, China lost its national autonomy in trade, customs, and legal jurisdiction. Finally, to add injury to insult, China was required to pay Britain 21 million taels (a traditional Chinese unit of weight) of silver as compensation for the opium destroyed by Chinese officials.

Concessions to the British encouraged demands from other foreign powers for equal treatment. As a consequence of a legal provision known as the "most-favored-nation" clause that was inserted into every treaty signed by China, Beijing's concessions granted to any foreign country would automatically be extended to all of them. In addition to Britain, the United States, France, Germany, Italy, Russia, Austria, and Japan all tried to partake of the spoils. Each demanded special concessions inside China and privileges for their traders and missionaries. Thus, for example, the British carved out a sphere of influence in the Yangtze Valley, France in the Bay of Guanzhou, Germany in Shantung, Japan in southern Manchuria, and Russia in northern Manchuria and outer Mongolia.

Under this pressure, China was in danger of being carved up into separate European colonies. Its political and economic autonomy was seriously eroded. For example, it had to agree to the stationing of foreign troops on Chinese soil and to allowing foreign gunboats unimpeded access to Chinese waterways. It also had to turn over to foreigners the collection of customs duties. In addition, foreign business interests were permitted to own or operate mines, railways, banks, and shipping and telecommunication companies.

To compound these problems, China lost a series of foreign wars imposed on it. As a result, it had to renounce its suzerainty over its traditional vassal states. During the period from 1875 to 1895, Burma, Annam, Tonkin, Mongolia, Korea, and the Ryukyus were detached from China's sphere of influence and subsequently became colonies and dependencies of the Europeans and Japanese. China's defeat by the Japanese in 1895 was a particularly shocking blow to the imperial dynasty. The ensuing Treaty of Shimonoseki severed Taiwan from China and made it into a Japanese colony. At the same time, China was required to pay 200 million taels of silver to Japan as war indemnity, when China's total annual government receipts were only 90 million taels. The Chinese government owed so much to foreigners that according to one estimate,[7] in 1899, 30 percent of its ordinary tax revenues went to pay those debts. According to another estimate, between 1842 and 1911, China was forced to pay indemnities to a foreign power on 110 separate occasions.[8] Thus, the Chinese were losing land and money as well as national autonomy.

It is perhaps not difficult to imagine that this chain of events contributed to antiforeign sentiments in China. Chinese nationalism was stimulated by the humiliating setbacks suffered at the hands of Western and Japanese imperialists. The unequal treaties created mass indignation and inspired popular demands to overthrow the decrepit Qing Dynasty (finally accomplished in 1911). Western gunboat diplomacy, the looting and sacking of the Imperial Palace, and the institutions of extraterritoriality and foreign concessions (where signs read "no dogs and Chinese allowed") provided the historical background for China's subsequent attempts to expel foreign influences from its soil.

Western and Japanese imperialism helped to awaken nationalist sentiments in other parts of the Pacific region as well. Japanese colonialism contributed to the rise of Korean nationalism. French and British colonialism aroused Vietnamese and Burmese nationalism. The struggles between the Asian nationalists and the foreign powers (as well as the native collaborators backed by these foreign powers) would later develop into several major wars (in China, Korea, and Vietnam) and insurrections (in Malaya and the Philippines) in the twentieth century.

In contrast to China, Japan was successful in building a strong army and economy during the final three decades of the nineteenth century. Japan also had to suffer the indignity of extraterritoriality and the loss of tariff autonomy to Westerners. These encroachments provided fodder for Japanese nationalism just as they did in China and in other parts of Asia. However, whereas China almost collapsed under the weight of foreign imperialism, Japan was able to recover from it. In 1899 it ended extraterritoriality, and in 1911 it regained control over tariffs. We have already considered the domestic reasons why Japan had greater success than China in managing the Western challenge. It is now necessary to mention a few foreign factors that helped Japan.

Before the 1850s, Westerners did not pay much attention to Japan. In comparison to the continental size of China, India, and Australia, Japan looked puny. The island nation did not seem to have nearly so much promise as a source of raw materials or as a market for manufactured exports. As a result, Japan was left relatively alone while the Westerners concentrated on dividing up the rest of the world. In short, Japan was not so tightly integrated into the capitalist world system as China was—as shown in the opium and tea trade. Nor did the Western capitalists try to capture the internal Japanese market, as they did in China, by taking over vital industries such as rails, banks, mines, utilities, and telecommunications. The control of these industries remained in Japanese hands. Consequently, whereas the Chinese were not able to undertake rapid economic development relatively free of foreign interference and control, the Japanese could do so.

Timing was critical. Although in the 1850s Japan was an easy target for Western predation, by the 1880s it had developed sufficient military and economic strength to discourage such behavior. The interim period gave Japan the vital breathing space to catch up, an opportunity that China did not have. Indeed, by the 1890s the Japanese were able to defeat the Chinese soundly in the battlefield. This turn of events had two consequences.[9] The huge Chinese war indemnity—amounting to about one-third of the Japanese gross national product at that time—provided the capital to further propel Japan's industrialization. Moreover, having proved its military capabilities, Japan now appeared as an eligible "junior partner" of Britain, which by the 1890s was looking for an Asian ally to check expanding Russian influence. It therefore had to be courted rather than conquered. Thus, the pursuit of military security and regional order by one country (Britain) had the consequence of fostering the national growth and autonomy of another country (Japan), even though this consequence might not have been clearly foreseen or fully intended by the former.

JAPANESE EXPANSIONISM
AND WORLD WAR II

It was Japan's misfortune that by the time it was ready to join the game of imperialist aggrandizement, the world had been pretty much carved up already. Instead of a far-flung empire, Japan had to settle for small territories nearby. Tokyo's attempts at expanding its colonial possessions beyond Korea and Taiwan ran into Western opposition. The British and the Americans were concerned about Japan's dominance in China. The Americans in 1899 promoted the idea of "open door" (that is, China should offer equal and unrestricted access to all foreign powers) as a means of checking the rising Japanese influence. Thus, imperialism was becoming unfashionable just when Japan was ready to participate. As a latecomer, it felt it was unjustly being denied its rightful place.

Like the primary interest of other colonial governments, the aim of Japan in Korea and Taiwan was to extract the economic surplus and to transfer it to the home islands. The principal exports of Korea were minerals, rice, and labor, and those of Taiwan were rice and sugar. In both cases, the Japanese colonial administration prevented political organization and economic entrepreneurship among the native people. For the purpose of more efficient exploitation of Korea's and Taiwan's resources, the Japanese introduced the necessary socioeconomic infrastructure. Roads and ports were built, schools were opened, surveys and registration of landed properties were undertaken, and tax codes were developed. Moreover, unlike the European colonialists, the Japanese brought some industries to Korea and Taiwan when it appeared that these colonies could assume an intermediate role for processing the raw materials from China and Southeast Asia. Finally, the Japanese developed a strong bureaucratic apparatus—especially a ubiquitous police force—to enforce political order and economic extraction. These Japanese legacies became the foundation for the subsequent development of an autocratic and strong state in South Korea and Taiwan after World War II. They also facilitated the industrialization efforts of these countries from the 1950s on.

The overthrow of the Qing Dynasty in 1911 did not immediately produce in its wake a unified or effective national government in China. Instead, this country suffered from chronic warfare among various regional warlords. In 1927, however, the Chinese Nationalist forces, under Chiang Kai-shek, successfully completed the Northern Expedition, which brought the warlords under greater control of the central government. China seemed to be headed for unification with a strong national authority. To Toyko it was obvious that this development, if unchecked, would thwart the imperialist ambitions of Japan. Therefore, the Japanese Kwantung Army decided to act quickly; in 1931 it took over Manchuria, the northeastern part of China. Then, in 1937, after fabricating the so-called Marco Polo Bridge incident, Japan invaded China and started a full-fledged war.

In the face of the Japanese assault, the Chinese Nationalist government withdrew to the interior. Coastal China, with its centers of commerce and industries, fell into Japanese hands. The withdrawal of the Chinese Nationalist forces left the Chinese Communists as the only major armed resistance group against the Japanese invaders in the occupied territories. The Communist guerrilla forces were able to gain military experience and political popularity in this armed struggle. Thus, the Japanese invasion had the effect of weakening the Chinese Nationalists and of extending a much needed breathing space to their Communist foes, who were to emerge at the end of the Sino-Japanese War with a large fighting force and substantial territorial control in north China. This is a rather ironic development—one of Toyko's stated justifications for its aggression against China was to combat the influence of communism.

In July 1941, the United States, sensing that the Japanese invasion would jeopardize other foreign interests in China and, more important, upset the regional balance in the Pacific, demanded that Tokyo give up its recent political and territorial gains. To give credibility to its demand, Washington imposed a trade embargo against Japan, denying it such important strategic materials as petroleum and scrap iron (which can be seen as a pre-OPEC use of economic sanctions as a means of advancing foreign policy goals). The U.S. embargo was joined by the British and the Dutch. They threatened to continue this embargo until Japan withdrew its troops from Indochina (which the Japanese had recently taken over from the French) and especially from China.

The Japanese militarists were unwilling to give up their hard-won gains in China, thereby surrendering Tokyo's claim to be a great power. Nor could they afford to wait out the embargo because Japan's strategic reserves were rapidly dwindling. In the absence of the necessary material support, the Imperial Navy could not maintain its combat effectiveness for more than eighteen months—after that, Japan would in effect be disarmed. At the same time, any attempt to obtain the desired strategic materials from Southeast Asia (especially British Malaya and Dutch East Indies) would risk a war with the United States—a country judged by Tokyo to be seven or eight times stronger than Japan. Thus, none of the policy options available to the Japanese leaders was palatable.

The Japanese were in a quandary. In their opinion, an attack against the European colonies in Southeast Asia would probably result in a declaration of war by the United States. Yet concessions to the U.S. demands and procrastination meant even more certain and unacceptable consequences. In the words of one analyst,[10] "The only escape from this dilemma was by blunting one of its horns—to accept war with the U.S., but to attempt it under circumstances where the chances of victory were higher." Japan thus decided to take the initiative by controlling the time and place of the initial hostility against the United States. Counting on the element of surprise, Japan attacked Pearl Harbor in December 1941.

In the immediate sense, the U.S. policy of deterrence had failed. Instead of discouraging further Japanese aggression in the Pacific region, the policy actually precipitated a Japanese attack against the United States. Thus the attempt to preserve the existing regional order had in the short run the opposite effect of creating more armed conflict and political upheaval. Of course, the Japanese were unable to win the war that they had started. After the United States dropped atomic bombs on Hiroshima and Nagasaki, the Japanese government surrendered unconditionally to the allies in 1945.

The war in the Pacific (1937–1945) did, however, have several important and lasting legacies. First, as mentioned earlier, the Japanese invasion had the unintended effect of boosting the strength and popularity of the Chinese Communist Party. Whereas in the early 1930s the Chinese Communists were constantly on the run in the face of the repeated armed onslaughts of the Nationalists, they had become a formidable military and political force by the mid-1940s. The ineffectual and repressive policies of the Nationalist government contributed to its declining popularity and to the rising stock of the Communists, led by Mao Zedong. In the ensuing Chinese Civil War, the Nationalist government, despite its larger and better-equipped army, was defeated. By 1949, that government had been driven to Taiwan (which had reverted to Chinese control after Japan's surrender in 1945). The victorious Communists established the People's Republic of China.

Second, the Pacific war had the effect of discrediting the Western colonial powers and of encouraging the rising tide of Asian nationalism. In the course of the war (especially in its early stages), British, French, Dutch, and, indeed, U.S. forces suffered some humiliating defeats at the hands of the Japanese, thereby helping to remove any illusions about European superiority over the Asians. Western colonial rulers in the Philippines, Hong Kong, Singapore, Malaya, Burma, Vietnam, and Indonesia were replaced by Japanese and native puppet administrators. After the war, the people of these countries were not about to welcome back their Western colonial masters. When the European governments tried to reimpose colonial rule, they encountered violent opposition in several places, such as Indonesia and Vietnam. The United States was thus forced to choose between its loyalty to Western allies and its commitment to the ideal of national self-determination.

Third, many conservative elements had become politically discredited as a result of their collaboration with the Japanese imperialists during the Pacific war. Perhaps even more important for the subsequent period of East Asian history, the Communists often led the resistance movement against the Japanese. At the end of the war, the Chinese, Vietnamese, and, to a lesser extent, the Korean and Malayan Communist parties were the bearers of popular nationalism. They also often possessed the most effectively organized political and military force in their respective countries. Thus, the stage was again set for the subsequent dilemma faced by the United States in dealing with Asian nationalism led by Communist parties.

Finally, the Pacific war brought about Japan's total devastation. At the war's end, Japan's economy and cities were in total shambles. It was estimated that one-third of its cities and two-thirds of its industries were totally destroyed. The country was subjected to military occupation by the U.S. forces under General Douglas MacArthur, who became Japan's supreme ruler. In order to ensure against a possible revival of militarism, the U.S. occupation authority proceeded to disband Japan's armed forces and its giant industrial-financial conglomerates (called *zaibatsu* in Japanese). Indeed, the United States quite literally drafted the current Japanese constitution, which pledges that Japan will never again resort to war. As we shall see later, these U.S.-inspired or U.S.-dictated reforms contributed to Japan's rapid economic recovery and its emergence as a formidable trade competitor.

U.S. HEGEMONY AND THE KOREAN WAR

The United States emerged from World War II as the world's most powerful country. Whereas the cities and industries of Western Europe, the USSR, Japan, and China lay in ruins, those of the United States had escaped the war undamaged. In fact, the U.S. economy was boosted by war production, so that by 1945 it accounted for almost half of the globe's economic output. Additionally, the United States had a monopoly on atomic weapons. No other country, or combination of countries, came close to its economic, military, and political power.

In Asia, U.S. influence was paramount. Japan was occupied and ruled by a U.S. military regime. In China, Washington's economic and military aid helped to sustain the Nationalist government, which had increasingly come under the pressure of Communist challenge. Korea, a former Japanese colony, was divided into two zones at the 38th parallel. In the southern zone, the United States took over control from the Japanese. Similarly, the USSR assumed control in the northern zone. This temporary division gave rise to the subsequent formation of rival Korean regimes. In Indochina and Southeast Asia, the United States played a supportive role in the transfer of power from the Japanese militarists to the European colonialists.

Although the United States had professed the ideals of national self-determination and liberal democracy in its fight against the fascist powers in World War II, it did not implement those ideals in the Pacific region after that struggle was over. In Indochina and Southeast Asia, nationalists—some of them, like Ho Chi Minh of Vietnam, happened also to be Communists—were demanding political independence for their countries. Britain, France, and the Netherlands wanted to reimpose their colonial control over these areas, and Washington often chose to support Western colonialism rather than Asian nationalism. This is not to say that U.S. officials did not feel a certain degree of ambivalence when faced with this policy dilemma or that they were steadfastly opposed to the forces of Asian nationalism (the Philippines, a U.S. colony, was granted independence). Nevertheless, in the minds of many policymakers in Washington, the emergent cold war against the USSR (Washington's ally in World War II) was a more important concern than European colonialism.

In China, at the end of World War II, the Nationalist government and the Communist insurgents were poised to resume civil war. The United States, even though occasionally professing its neutrality in this struggle, actually lent enormous tangible as well as intangible aid to the Nationalists. For example, U.S. transports rushed Nationalist soldiers to Manchuria so that the Communists would be denied the control of territories being surrendered by the Japanese. In addition, the United States continued its economic and military assistance to the Nationalist government. The latter's principal domestic supporters were the landlord class and the rich merchants of Shanghai, who were the target of the peasant-based revolution led by the Communists. Consequently, the United States was increasingly identified with the conservative social elements and the wealthy capitalist class in China. This pattern was repeated in South Korea and, later, again in South Vietnam. Washington became in effect the champion of the large landowners, rich financiers, and top bureaucrats—many of whom, ironically, had also been prominent collaborators of the Japanese militarists.

It became clear in the latter half of the 1940s that the struggle between the United States and the USSR had intensified. Pro-Soviet elements had taken over the governments of East European countries and, in the words of Winston Churchill, an "iron curtain" had fallen over these countries. To counter the perceived threat of Soviet expansion, the United States initiated the Marshall Plan and later, the North Atlantic Treaty Organization (NATO). The Marshall Plan offered massive U.S. funding to help the economic recovery of the West European countries and to dampen the electoral popularity of their Communist parties (which enjoyed an especially large following in France and Italy). For its part, NATO provided the legal basis and the organizational means for the United States to extend military protection to Western Europe in the event of a possible Soviet invasion.

Washington tended to interpret Asian developments through the prism of the intensifying cold war in Europe. The defeat of the Nationalists by the Communists in China (1949) became a cause for grave concern because the emergent Sino-Soviet alliance seemed to give the Communists control of the Eurasian land mass stretching from the Baltic Sea to the South China Sea. U.S. officials became preoccupied with the threat of a monolithic Communist bloc under the control and direction of Moscow.

In June 1950, North Korean forces attacked the southern zone in a bid to reunify Korea under the Communist regime that had been established in the northern zone. In response, President Harry Truman ordered the 7th Fleet to "neutralize" the Taiwan Strait—that is, to prevent an impending Chinese Communist attempt to take over Taiwan. By this act, the United States saved the Chinese Nationalist government on the island from imminent demise; it also perpetuated, to this day, the confrontation between the two sides in the Chinese Civil War. At the same time, the United States intervened militarily in the Korean civil war under the pretext that North Korea had committed international aggression against South Korea. Technically, of course, North and South Korea were not two independent countries but rather two zones of the same country (the zones having been set up to administer the Japanese surrender to U.S. and Soviet authorities).

The U.S. intervention in Korea was endorsed by a resolution of the United Nations (UN), in which Washington and its West European allies were dominant. At the time of the outbreak of the Korean War, the Soviet Union was boycotting the United Nations because that world organization had refused to admit the Communist PRC government as the legitimate representative of China (Beijing did not gain admission until 1972). This Soviet absence made it possible for the United States to push through UN approval for the Korean intervention (had Moscow's representatives been present, they could have exercised their veto power in the Security Council). This intervention in turn put the United States and the PRC on a collision course and ensured their mutual hostility until the early 1970s—to the obvious benefit of Moscow.

More specifically, the U.S. and South Korean forces under UN auspices were able to turn back the North Korean attack and, indeed, to assume the offensive. Under the leadership of MacArthur, they crossed the 38th parallel with the goal of uniting Korea under a pro-U.S. government. By October 1950, the UN forces were at the Yalu River (the border between the PRC and Korea), and the North Korean government was on the verge of collapse. This development raised grave concern in Beijing. It would be as if Washington was faced with a Soviet army marching toward the Rio Grande, pledging to install an anti-American government in Mexico. Indeed, from Beijing's perspective, the situation seemed even more ominous than just the prospect of having to live with a hostile regime at its doorstep would warrant. General MacArthur was threatening to "roll back" communism in Asia, suggesting that the U.S. forces might invade the PRC.

The Beijing government warned the United States that it would intervene in the Korean conflict if Washington did not cease its invasion of North Korea. This warning was ignored by Washington. In November 1950, Chinese "volunteers" attacked MacArthur's forces and drove them back to the 38th parallel. The military stalemate that ensued lasted until July 1953, when an armistice was signed.

The Korean War was a watershed event in the recent history of the Pacific region. It consolidated the Sino-Soviet alliance, as Beijing had to seek Soviet support to counter the U.S. threat. It also finalized the Sino-American rift, which was not repaired until President Richard Nixon's visit to the PRC in 1972. Moreover, the Korean War precipitated the extension to Asia of the U.S. **containment policy,** whereby Washington erected a system of bilateral and multilateral treaties to prevent the spread of Communist influence. In short, this conflict helped to demarcate the opposing patterns of political, economic, and military alignment in the Pacific region for the next two decades or so.

To shore up its anti-Communist allies, Washington provided them with massive economic and military aid. Except for the U.S. aid to South Vietnam during the Vietnam War, Taiwan and South Korea were the two major East Asian beneficiaries of Washington's largess. According to one estimate,[11] Taiwan received $5.6 billion (about $425 for each Taiwanese) and South Korea received $13 billion (or $600 per capita). In contrast, all of Latin America and all of Africa had only been given $3.2 billion in U.S. military aid between 1945 and 1978. The U.S. aid to its Asian allies was essential for propping up the latter's governments and economies. This aid also gave Washington the necessary leverage to encourage various social and economic reforms—such as land redistribution, currency adjustment, trade liberalization, and an outward-looking economic strategy of emphasizing exports—that helped to lay the groundwork for the subsequent rapid development of Taiwan and South Korea.

The Korean War also precipitated a revision of Washington's view of Japan. Instead of treating Japan as a defeated enemy whose military resurgence had to be guarded against at all costs, the United States began to elevate Japan to the role of a junior partner in the struggle against communism. The breakup of the *zaibatsu* was moderated and put on hold. Japan's Liberal Democratic Party—in spite of its name, a conservative party—was cultivated. With the help of the U.S. occupation authority, leftist politicians and bureaucrats were purged from influential posts. The labor unions were subjected to tightened regulation. Moreover, with the encouragement of the United States, a national "police force" was introduced, even though Japan was supposed to be demilitarized. This force was subsequently enlarged and modernized, again with U.S. help, to become Japan's armed forces. Finally, the Korean War came at a propitious time for Japan's moribund economy, which was given a much needed boost as a result of the U.S. military expenditures.

The civil wars of China and Korea left another lasting legacy in terms of domestic U.S. politics. The victory of Mao Zedong in China and the military stalemate in Korea provided fodder for an acrimonious partisan debate. Right-wing Republicans charged that Communist sympathizers within the U.S. government were responsible for the "loss of China." The intimidation tactics and false accusations of these demagogues, especially those of Senator Joseph McCarthy (from whose name the term *McCarthyism* was derived), smeared reputations and ruined careers. Yet such tactics also proved that partisan political advantages might be gained by charging one's political opponent with being "soft on communism." At the same time, an inability to bring the Korean War to a quick and successful conclusion apparently cost Truman his popularity and the Democratic Party the White House (lost to Republican war hero Dwight Eisenhower). Memories of these events and the lessons drawn from them were to have an important impact later on U.S. decision making during the Vietnam War.

THE VIETNAM WAR
AND THE SINO-SOVIET BREAK

Analyzed in retrospect, the Vietnam War marked the beginning of the relative decline of U.S. influence in the world. While Washington was preoccupied with this conflict, the Soviets were strengthening their strategic stockpile and the Japanese were building their industrial structure. In this sense, the cost of the Vietnam War for the United States went far beyond the lives that were lost, the money that was spent, and the political reputations that were compromised. The war sapped the country's economic vitality, eroded its military superiority, and raised doubts about its political judgment. The U.S. leadership position in the world accordingly suffered.

To understand the Vietnam conflict, one must remember the situtation at the end of World War II. After the defeat of the Japanese in 1945, the French sought to reimpose their colonial rule in Indochina. This effort was supported by the United States but violently opposed by the Vietnamese Communists (called Viet Minh), led by Ho Chi Minh. In the ensuing armed struggle, the French were defeated. The climax of the war came in 1954 when the French garrison outpost at Dien Bien Phu was overrun. Shortly thereafter, a conference of the major world powers—including the United States, the USSR, Britain, and the PRC— was held in Geneva to end the war.

The Geneva Accord, which emerged from this conference, established a cease-fire between the combatants. As a temporary measure, Vietnam was partitioned into two zones at the 17th parallel. The north was to be controlled by the Communist Viet Minh, and the south was to be ruled by the French-backed Emperor Bao Dai. Both zones were barred from entering into foreign alliances. The agreement also stipulated that a national election was to be held in 1956 for the purpose of reunifying Vietnam.

In its essence, the Geneva Accord included these terms: The French would be given a graceful exit; the Viet Minh would not pursue their military advantages; and in exchange for a cease-fire, the Communists were promised a national election, which they were expected to win easily (President Eisenhower estimated that Ho Chi Minh would win by a landslide, capturing 80 percent of the votes). However, when the "decent interval" negotiated by the parties had passed, the South Vietnamese government—with the support of the United States—refused to hold national election. In the eyes of the North Vietnamese, this refusal invalidated the other parts of the package deal. They were then entitled to disregard the cease-fire and the demarcation line at the 17th parallel and to resume the civil war. To the United States and South Vietnam, however, this resumption of hostilities was tantamount to international aggression by one country against another.

The U.S. decision-making process in the Vietnam War was fraught with contradictions. On the one hand, each succeeding U.S. president did not want to lose a country to communism during "his watch." The conservative backlash stemming from the bitter "who lost China" debate suggested the political hazards of being "soft on communism." On the other hand, the presidents were mindful of the wrath that U.S. voters had directed against Truman and the Democrats as a result of the Korean War. The Chinese intervention in Korea had increased the war's human and financial cost, and the possibility of Soviet intervention there had threatened to raise the stakes further. The U.S. electorate, not liking the mounting price tag (in blood, sweat, tears, and dollars), had turned to Eisenhower to "clean up the mess."

Thus, successive U.S. administrations were caught in a dilemma. To allow South Vietnam to fall into Communist hands would exact an electoral penalty. But to engage in a protracted and costly war with either of the Communist giants would also risk the public's displeasure. Therefore, as one student of the Vietnam War argued, every U.S. president settled for stalemate.[12] That is, instead of trying to win the war and thereby risk the danger of Chinese intervention, the aim of each president was not to lose the war. Rather than to defeat the Vietnamese Communists, the objective was to prevent them from winning. Only in this light can one explain Washington's puzzling behavior of choosing neither victory (which it had the means to achieve) nor withdrawal. For about two decades, this U.S. policy actually succeeded (that is, it did prevent the collapse of the Saigon government), albeit at a tremendous human, financial, and political cost. It was only after the Watergate scandal that a more assertive Congress in 1975 finally terminated the U.S. involvement.

In hindsight, it is ironic that successive U.S. administrations had justified Washington's Vietnam involvement on the grounds of checking the expansion of Sino-Soviet influence in Asia. Hanoi was perceived to be under the influence of Beijing, whose actions were in turn supposedly directed by Moscow. However, U.S. combat involvement in the Vietnam conflict (in 1964) had actually been preceded by a deepening and increasingly public schism between the PRC and the Soviet Union. The Chinese Communists accused Soviet Premier Nikita Khrushchev of revising orthodox Marxist-Leninist ideology and of pursuing peaceful coexistence with the United States. Beijing urged worldwide armed revolution, or wars of national liberation, against the United States and its local allies. Indeed, the gravity of the Sino-Soviet dispute had caused Moscow to pull its advisers out of the PRC in the early 1960s, an action that in turn aroused significant Chinese resentment. The escalating Vietnam War in the mid- and late 1960s further exacerbated the friction between the two Communist giants, with Moscow counseling Hanoi to pursue the diplomatic track and Beijing advocating the opposite course of militant armed struggle.[13]

By the late 1960s and the early 1970s, the Chinese and the Soviets had fought several border skirmishes that together resulted in hundreds of casualties. Both sides amassed troops and armaments along their extensive borders. There were even rumors that Moscow was considering a preemptive strike against China's nuclear installations. It was during this tense period that a delicate courtship, through Pakistani intermediaries, was started between the United States and the PRC. Washington and Beijing were both concerned about the danger of Soviet expansionism and sought to use the other country to contain Moscow's influence. The climax of the Sino-American rapprochement came when President Richard Nixon visited Beijing in 1972. In December 1978, President Jimmy Carter announced U.S. diplomatic recognition of the PRC, thus normalizing the relations between Washington and Beijing after a break of thirty years.

During the course of the Vietnam War, North Vietnamese sanctuaries and supply lines (the so-called Ho Chi Minh trails) were moved increasingly into Laos and Cambodia in order to escape U.S. interdiction efforts. At the same time, U.S. ground and aerial campaigns designed to destroy them moved as well into Laotian and Cambodian territories. Thus, these two Indochinese states were also engulfed by a war that eventually led to Communist takeover.

However, the Cambodian Communists (known as the Khmer Rouge) and the Vietnamese Communists were soon involved in a bitter dispute. This dispute escalated into the outright Vietnamese invasion of Cambodia that deposed the ruthless Pol Pot regime and installed in its place a pro-Vietnamese government. Because Beijing backed the Pol Pot regime, the Chinese retaliated by attacking Vietnam in a month-long campaign in 1979. Although limited in military success, Beijing's action elicited the predictable warnings from Moscow in support of its Vietnamese ally (which expelled thousands of its own citizens of Chinese origin). Ironically, the United States had fought the Vietnam War ostensibly to prevent the expansion of a monolithic Communist bloc. It can hardly be said that the Communist victories in Indochina contributed to the cohesion or solidarity among countries professing official adherence to this ideology. If anything, they had precisely the opposite effect.

There was yet another irony of the Vietnam War. Earlier we noted that U.S. military spending for the Korean War gave the Japanese economy a much needed boost. The Vietnam War served the same function in helping the economic takeoff of Taiwan and especially South Korea. Therefore, the military sacrifices of the United States in these conflicts contributed in a sense to the rise of its East Asian trade competitors.

As an additional irony, the Vietnam War as well as the Korean War were fought by Washington not only to keep "China out" but also to keep "Japan in." That is to say, the U.S. involvement in these two conflicts was very much premised on a concern for the possible political and military reverberations that Communist victories (especially on the Korean peninsula, given its proximity to Japan) could cause in Tokyo.

Would Japan lose confidence in the United States and react by either assuming a neutralist foreign policy posture or pursuing an independent military capability? This scenario was as much a nightmare for Washington as was the prospect of Chinese expansionism. Thus, in 1954, Eisenhower remarked that the loss of "Indochina . . . would take away the region Japan must have as a trading area, or it would force Japan to turn toward China and Manchuria, or towards the Communist areas in order to live. The consequences of the loss of Japan to the free world are just incalculable."[14] The final irony of the Vietnam War is that by the early 1970s (even before the North Vietnamese troops marched into Saigon in 1975), Washington was already aligning itself with Beijing to oppose the Soviets and, at the same time, pressuring Tokyo to increase its defense spending.

CONCLUSION

After the turbulence of the 1960s and 1970s, the Pacific region entered a more tranquil and stable period. The relations among the PRC, Japan, and the United States are probably more cordial now, at the beginning of the 1990s, than at any time in recent memory. With the visit by Soviet leader Mikhail Gorbachev to Beijing in spring 1989, Sino-Soviet relations also seemed to be entering a more stable and less acrimonious period. Similarly, dialogue between the Chinese and the Vietnamese has taken place on problems of mutual interest. There have even been some cultural and commercial exchanges between the PRC on the one hand, and Taiwan and South Korea on the other. In short, whereas lingering problems persist in some bilateral relations (e.g., the status of Taiwan in Sino-American relations, the status of Cambodia in Sino-Vietnamese relations, the problem of trade balance and protectionism in U.S.-Japanese relations), there has clearly been a trend toward détente, or the relaxation of international tension.

There has also been a general movement toward greater personal freedom and electoral contest in countries such as Taiwan, South Korea, and the Philippines. The overthrow of Ferdinand Marcos in particular ushered in an era of more democratic politics in the Philippines. The one significant blot on the record of democratic development in this area was the Chinese crackdown against Beijing demonstrators in June 1989. This repression forced legitimate dissent underground and turned back the clock on political liberalization.

Finally, the Pacific Rim countries have shown a great deal of economic vitality. Japan's economic success is well known. Its footsteps are being followed by South Korea, Taiwan, and Singapore—all of which are rapidly closing the economic gap between them and the developed countries. Their economic successes are being imitated by Thailand, Malaysia, the Philippines, Indonesia, and even the PRC. The latter countries are positioning themselves to take over the labor-intensive industries that once provided the locomotive for the rapid growth of Taiwan and South Korea. In short, as we enter the 1990s, the Pacific Basin seems to be developing into a more peaceful, democratic, and prosperous region.

THREE

□ □ □

Convergent Goals, Divergent Conduct

The values of economic growth, political order, and military security are almost universally shared. This consensus, however, belies three perennial challenges to policy attempts aimed at maintaining or enhancing these values. First, there exists a variety of theoretical perspectives that give discrepant advice about the most appropriate and efficacious ways to attain these values. Instead of a single magic formula, policymakers have to contend with and choose from many *competing strategies* in their pursuit of the goals of growth, order, and security.

Second, the pursuit of these goals by each country can have important consequences abroad. If not properly managed, it can intensify international competition (for example, arms race, trade war) because of the perception that one country's gains necessarily become another country's losses (a situation described by political scientists as a *zero-sum game*). According to this perception, a militarily strong United States suggests a more vulnerable Soviet Union; similarly, successful Japanese exports pose a competitive threat to existing U.S. industries. By the same token, the economic, political, or military weakness of one country can affect others, as when economic recession or political disorder spreads among trade partners and geographic neighbors. The management of such cross-national *ripple effects* is an essential part of statecraft.

Third, it is sometimes difficult to pursue growth, order, and security all at the same time. Indeed, policies aimed at achieving one value may have the undesirable side effect of undermining another value, such as when rapid economic growth brought in its wake political disorder in the PRC. As another example, the United States has had to pay an economic price in the form of forgone growth because of its high defense spending and overseas military commitments. In short, public officials must attend to possible *trade-offs* in designing and executing national policies.

In this chapter, I shall focus on the competing strategies adopted by particular members of the Pacific community in their pursuit of the individual goals of growth, order, and security. In Chapter 4, I shall attend to these countries' management of the trade-offs among these goals. Both chapters will address the domestic and foreign ramifications of particular policy courses. In combination, these three concerns—the need to choose among competing strategies, to manage value trade-offs, and to balance domestic and foreign considerations—are the essence of persistent policy dilemmas.

PRODUCTION PACKAGE AND PACKAGING

Economic production entails a combination of factors, including capital, labor, technology, raw materials, and management supervision. In addition, a production site and a market for finished products are necessary. Together, these ingredients constitute a production package. When one or more of these ingredients is missing, economic production and growth are stifled.

Because of nature or history, the distribution of these production factors is uneven across the globe. Some countries have plenty of natural resources (think of the mineral wealth of Canada and Soviet Siberia), whereas other countries have plenty of cheap labor (e.g., the large population of the PRC). Still other countries, such as the United States and Japan, are endowed with advanced technology, abundant capital, or large consumer markets. Thus, countries have different **comparative advantages** (economic assets that enable them to produce a good more efficiently than others can) in their command of the various ingredients necessary for economic production and growth.

Much of the debate about alternative development strategies stems from this fundamental fact. To what extent should a country recruit foreign ingredients to make up for its domestic shortfall in one or more of production ingredients, and to what extent should a country rely on its own efforts to overcome these shortfalls? What are the relative advantages and disadvantages of an outward-looking development strategy in comparison to those of an inward-looking development strategy? To what extent should the government let market forces determine the cross-national exchange of goods and production factors, and to what extent should it intervene in this exchange? These questions in turn depend on one's assessment of the relative bargaining power of and the distribution of benefits and costs among those countries involved in an exchange relationship.

Classical economists generally favor an outward-looking development strategy. In particular, the nineteenth-century English economist David Ricardo, was very influential in promoting the idea of comparative advantage.[1] He used the exchange of Portuguese wine for English linen to illustrate the virtues of free trade. Portugal had some unique advantages (soil, climate, traditional expertise) in the production of wine, whereas England enjoyed favorable conditions for the production of linen. If each country specialized in what it could do better, both wine and linen could be produced more efficiently. The supply of these goods would increase, and their price would fall. English consumers would benefit because they could buy wine from Portugal more cheaply than if this commodity had to be produced in England. Similarly, Portuguese consumers would benefit from cheaper and more plentiful linen.

The exchange of English linen for Portuguese wine in the above example does not require government coordination but is instead left to the market forces of supply and demand. These forces are reflected in the prices for English linen and Portuguese wine. Because England could produce linen more efficiently than Portugal, its linen was cheaper than Portuguese linen. This price differential would encourage the demand for English linen and discourage the demand for Portuguese linen, a development that would in turn influence the future supply of linen produced in these two countries. Thus, the prices emerging from the voluntary transactions between buyers and sellers in a free market help to promote collective efficiency and well-being for all concerned.[2]

The efficacy of the market and the benefits of free trade based on comparative advantage have been challenged by some analysts. One group of them subscribes to the **dependency theory,** which argues that Third World countries are highly dependent on the capital, technology, and markets of developed countries, that this dependence results in the exploitation and domination of the former by the latter, and that this exploitation and domination have in turn been responsible for the underdevelopment of Third World countries. Thus international exchanges of goods and production factors are highly asymmetrical, or unequal. Some countries are in a stronger bargaining position than others and can therefore derive more benefits from these exchanges than those in a weaker bargaining position. Typically, those who control capital and technology are the price makers, whereas those who provide labor and raw materials are the price takers. In this context, an international division of labor based on comparative advantage legitimizes and institutionalizes the exploitation and domination of the developing countries by the developed countries. The developing countries, given their abundance of labor and natural resources, are supposed to be "hewers of wood and drawers of water" and the developed countries are supposed to specialize in the more lucrative industrial and manufacturing processes.

This dependency perspective is quite popular in the Third World, especially in Latin America. The officials of many developing countries feel that a dependence on foreign capital, technology, market, and management expertise tends to distort or impair economic development and undermine political autonomy. Therefore, they advocate a policy of regulating, restricting, and perhaps even barring the entry of foreign capital, technology, and management into their economy. At the same time, they urge a policy of **import substitution,** an inward-looking strategy by which a country tries to reduce its reliance on foreign goods by developing its domestic capability of producing these goods.

The classical arguments about comparative advantage and free trade have also been criticized by analysts who adopt the **statist theory.** Advocates of statist theory argue that the governments or states of the late-industrializing countries must play an active role in guiding and promoting economic development. These statist scholars are skeptical about the efficacy of market forces in the late-industrializing countries and in their dealings with the industrialized countries. The active role of the government is necessary in order to offset the relatively weak entrepreneurial impulses and bargaining positions of the native bour- geoisie and to overcome various imperfections and distortions in the economic market. Some states have regulated the entry and departure of key production factors (e.g., capital, technology), whereas others have directly managed and operated key strategic industries (e.g., steel, pe- troleum). Still other states have assumed the responsibility of mobilizing and allocating the society's production resources according to a master economic plan.

The Pacific region features a variety of policy styles and conduct along several dimensions. One such dimension refers to the relative size of the private and the public sectors. Another dimension has to do with reliance on the market relative to reliance on government planning as a means of coordinating economic activities. Still a third dimension concerns the emphasis placed on an inward-looking strategy of economic development based on domestic production factors, as opposed to an outward-looking strategy based on acquisition of conducive foreign inputs (to offset domestic shortfalls in particular production factors). In socialist countries (e.g., the PRC, North Korea), the public sector (government- owned and -operated enterprises) dominates over the private sector (privately owned and operated enterprises). Conversely, in capitalist countries (e.g., Japan, Canada, the United States) the reverse is true; the means of economic production are overwhelmingly in private control, and business profits and losses are accrued or borne by individuals. As a second distinction, socialist countries rely predominantly on central planning by the government to allocate resources, set production targets, and regulate prices, whereas the capitalist countries depend primarily on market mechanisms (especially prices) to perform these functions. Finally, the socialist countries tend to be more inward looking, although not all capitalist countries are necessarily outward looking.

The above distinctions, however, should not be overdrawn. Pure cases of one ideal type or another rarely exist. Indeed, as we shall see in subsequent sections, one major reason for the economic dynamism and commercial adaptability of the East Asian countries involves their ability to combine effectively the desirable features from several seemingly divergent models or approaches. Thus, Japan, South Korea, Taiwan, and, most recently, the PRC, have all featured aspects of central planning and market competition, and public enterprises and private entrepreneurship. They have also shown alternating emphasis on import substitution and export expansion during the past forty years.

IMPORT SUBSTITUTION
VERSUS EXPORT EXPANSION

It is now commonplace to hear the economic successes of the capitalist East Asian countries explained in terms of their choice of **export expansion,** an outward-looking strategy that emphasizes foreign trade as a way of promoting domestic economic growth. Conversely, the less glowing economic performances of countries such as Brazil, Mexico, India, and the PRC have been attributed to their supposed reliance on a strategy of import substitution. In reality, these different strategies provide only a partial explanation.

Interestingly, despite their divergent political ideologies and economic development levels, the PRC, Japan, Korea, and Taiwan had a great deal in common in the early 1950s. They had all suffered grievously from the devastation of foreign and civil war. Much of their economy lay in waste, with production falling far short of prewar levels. Moreover, each country was torn away from its traditional markets and sources of capital and raw materials. Korea and Taiwan were rather abruptly severed from the Japanese empire as a result of Tokyo's defeat in World War II. This event was followed in short order by the partition of Korea into two rival zones and the detachment of Taiwan from the PRC. In all three cases, U.S. military intervention was the proximate cause.

Until the 1960s, the governments of the PRC, Taiwan, and South Korea pursued a similar development strategy. They all engaged in the first, or easy, stage of import substitution. That is, they all sought to replace imports of nondurable consumer goods—such as clothing and household items—by indigenous production. The manufacture of these nondurable consumer goods was labor intensive and not capital or technology intensive. Such manufacture suited the prevailing conditions of these countries (a shortage of capital and technology, but an abundance of cheap and unskilled workers). In terms of the production package, this first stage of import substitution also did not entail large management staffs or complex production or distribution networks. Instead, the commodities could be produced in relatively small, rudimentary factories and sold to the local market. Being cut off from their traditional supply sources, these East Asian countries made a virtue out of a necessity.

Starting from a depressed production level owing to wartime disruptions, the PRC, Taiwan, and South Korea all achieved high rates of economic growth during the 1950s. Their experiences were aided by two factors. In each country, rural reform stimulated a rapid increase in agricultural productivity; the surplus from this increased productivity was in turn channeled into the industrial sector to fuel the latter's growth. Each country also received substantial foreign aid in the form of capital, equipment, commodities, and advisers. Massive U.S. aid helped Taiwan and South Korea to offset their trade deficits and to sustain their high rates of investment. The Soviet Union extended economic assistance to the PRC, often in the form of large projects intended to improve the latter's communication infrastructure and heavy industrial foundation.

By the 1960s, all three East Asian countries had completed the easy phase of import substitution. Their developmental paths diverged sharply. Partly under the pressure of U.S. advisers, Taiwan and then South Korea initiated a series of economic reforms that eventually produced an export-oriented growth strategy. They brought their respective exchange rates to a more realistic level than before, offered easy credit and other subsidies to companies in the export business, and pursued foreign capital and technology that would enhance their export competitiveness. To facilitate the latter goal, they set up special economic zones where foreign companies could manufacture goods for export under very favorable conditions (low rent, low wages, low tariffs for imported raw materials, low taxes for business profits). Stressing their comparative advantage in an abundant, cheap, and malleable work force, these countries (as well as Hong Kong and Singapore) found a favorable niche in the export of light-industrial, labor-intensive products, such as textiles, shoes, and toys, to the markets of developed countries.

In contrast, even in the late 1950s, the PRC began to take a decisive turn toward the second stage of import substitution. In this phase a country aspires to achieve national self-sufficiency in the production of consumer durables (e.g., automobiles, refrigerators) and of the intermediate goods (e.g., steel, chemicals) that are necessary to manufacture those consumer durables. The second stage has proven to be quite challenging for most developing countries, and this was true also for the PRC. This stage requires large capital outlays, advanced technologies, and complex industrial organization and management coordination—precisely those elements of the production package that are usually in severe shortage in the developing countries. To acquire those scarce production factors, the PRC exported primary goods (food, minerals) to the Soviet Union in exchange for loans, technology, and advisers. However, instead of improving the PRC's economic autonomy, this exchange can be seen in retrospect as having exacerbated the PRC's foreign dependence. In the early 1960s, Moscow abruptly recalled its advisers from the PRC (along with the blueprints for projects being built with Soviet aid) as punishment in the deepening ideological dispute between these two Communist countries. Coming at the heels of three years of natural disasters in the PRC, this Soviet action vastly increased Beijing's economic hardship.

Since the 1960s, Taiwan's and South Korea's export-oriented economies have grown by leaps and bounds, and they are now poised to join the club of developed countries in both average living standards and industrial competitiveness. Clearly, these countries have undergone rapid and sustained upward mobility in the international system, a record that sets them apart from the rest of the Third World. Thus, for example, average income in Taiwan has risen to about U.S. $7,500 (from a low of U.S. $153 in 1952), and the island holds the second largest reserve of foreign currency in the world (about U.S. $75 billion in 1989, an amount surpassed only by Japan's). Taiwan's and South Korea's economic policies and developmental histories have followed the Japanese model. Indeed, the pattern of flying geese (where industrial laggards follow in the footsteps of the industrial leaders) has been used as an analogy to describe the tendency by these late industrializers to follow and imitate their Japanese predecessor.

Neoclassical economists see Taiwan's and South Korea's success as primarily the result of economic practices that conform to the market, in particular the adoption of an outward-looking export strategy. This success is often juxtaposed against the less glowing records of those capitalist and socialist countries (e.g., India, Mexico, Brazil, and the PRC) that have adopted an inward-looking strategy of import substitution. The capital, technology, and organization required by the second stage of import substitution have been the stumbling blocks for developing countries. In addition, capital- and technology-intensive projects are likely to decrease rather than increase the demand for unskilled labor—the one production factor that is in abundance in developing countries.

Moreover, the efficient production of intermediate industrial goods typically requires large plants and high volumes; yet, the domestic demand for such products in the developing countries is usually quite limited.

Thus, these countries are unable to take advantage of the *economies of scale* (by which the cost per unit of production tends to decline with increases in the volume of production). Similarly, low domestic demand in the developing countries raises the cost of producing consumer durables and reduces their variety. It also limits the number of and competition among indigenous producers, with the resulting sellers' market in turn adversely affecting the quality of products. These products are shielded from foreign competition by massive government subsidies and trade barriers. For these reasons, neoclassical economists tend to see attempts at second-stage import substitution by the developing countries as misguided because such attempts result in an inefficient allocation of production resources. These attempts, according to neoclassical economists, distort prices and ignore cross-national differences in comparative advantage (or disadvantage).

Neoclassical economists favor instead an export-oriented growth strategy. Such a strategy is seen to offer the advantages of maximizing a country's comparative advantage in particular product niches, stimulating domestic technological improvements through the forces of international competition, and exploiting the economies of scale. One well-known advocate of this strategy of growth has argued that "exporting involves 'extending a lower step on the staircase' by increasing the production of commodities in which the country has a comparative advantage, with low domestic resource costs per unit of foreign exchange."[3] This export orientation permits fuller utilization of the existing production capacities and thus enables more rapid increases in production output. Conversely, second-stage import substitution involves "traveling up the staircase," whereby the costs of producing domestic goods increasingly exceed the costs of purchasing the equivalent foreign goods on the international market.

Whereas it is quite true that the export-oriented capitalist economies of East Asia (namely, Japan, Taiwan, South Korea, Hong Kong, and Singapore) have achieved higher rates of economic growth than those capitalist as well as socialist countries pursuing a strategy of import substitution, it would be a vast oversimplification to explain the former's economic accomplishments only in terms of their outward-looking orientation. In the first place, the switch from first-stage import substitution to export expansion by the East Asian NICs (newly industrializing countries) has perhaps as much to do with historical timing, geographic reality, and political necessity as with policy foresight. As in the case of South Korea and Taiwan, the breakup of the Malaysian federation threatened to disrupt the long-standing trade ties between Singapore and its "economic hinterland" (Malaya). The internal markets of Singapore's and Hong Kong's entrepôt economies were even smaller than those of South Korea and Taiwan. Therefore, second-stage import substitution was quite simply infeasible for them.

For South Korea and Taiwan in the 1960s, the need for economic adjustments in view of the upcoming termination of U.S. aid and the concomitant heavy lobbying by U.S. economic advisers further encouraged the outward economic turn. In this regard, the so-called four little tigers (South Korea, Taiwan, Singapore, and Hong Kong) really only made a virtue out of necessity. They were also quite lucky because the field of NICs pushing exports to the developed countries was not nearly so crowded then (in the 1960s) as today. Moreover, a booming world economy, a relatively open (nonprotectionist) trade regime, and massive U.S. regional spending related to the Vietnam War all helped to launch the economic takeoff of these countries.

A simple dichotomy between the import-substitution and the export-expansion strategies would also be misleading. As a matter of fact, South Korea and, to a lesser extent, Taiwan have also pursued second-stage import substitution since the 1970s. Under the military regime of Park Chung-hee, Seoul organized a drive to develop South Korea's steel and chemical industries. This drive was in part motivated by a strong desire to create an indigenous base for heavy armament because Seoul was becoming increasingly apprehensive about its national security in the wake of the U.S. defeat in Vietnam and in the face of a possible decision by Washington to withdraw its troops from South Korea. To finance its ambitious plan to develop an indigenous capacity for intermediate products, Seoul borrowed heavily from foreign lenders. Mismanagement of this plan resulted in wasteful investments, surplus production capacity, rising inflation, and an overextended financial system. The energy crisis of 1979–1980 further upset this industrial drive, and the ensuing inflationary spiral and economic recession for a while threatened to derail South Korea's economic growth (its gross national product declined 5 percent in 1980). This economic setback resulted in considerable political tension, which contributed to Park's assassination. The Taiwanese government, although it did not promote industrial deepening with the same vigor and heavy-handedness as the South Korean government had, has also sought to develop and sustain public enterprises in such strategic sectors as energy, petrochemicals, and steel.

Just as the ostensibly outward-looking economies of South Korea and Taiwan have pursued selective aspects of second-stage import substitution, the ostensibly inward-looking economy of the socialist PRC made a turn outward after the disastrous years of the Cultural Revolution, with its accompanying political turmoil and economic stagnation. Beginning in the late 1970s, the successors of Mao Zedong sought to liberalize the economy. Under the leadership of Deng Xiaoping, the Beijing government launched the Four Modernizations plan. To achieve the major goal of this plan, modernization of the Chinese economy, Beijing undertook a series of reforms to deemphasize central planning and to encourage local initiative. Private plots and free markets were institutionalized in the countryside, and small private enterprises (restaurants, repair shops) blossomed in the cities. In addition, the PRC opened its doors to foreign investment, technology, and trade. It established special economic zones, where foreign businesses could form joint ventures with the Chinese. These business operations were primarily in the light industries (e.g., the manufacturing of bicycles, toys, clothing, shoes), whose products were intended for export. To promote its burgeoning foreign trade, Beijing hosted an increasing number of trade fairs and foreign businesspeople. This foreign trade (as well as tourism) has become an important source of income to finance the import of foreign technology and equipment needed for the PRC's industrial modernization. Indeed, the PRC's import of foreign goods has been rising at a much faster pace than its exports, thus accounting for its increasingly large trade deficits in the recent years.

Naturally, the recent economic reforms in the PRC do not indicate that somehow this country has decided to follow the footsteps of Taiwan and South Korea in pursuing export expansion as a means of economic growth. For one thing, the PRC's domestic market is far larger than that of its smaller neighbors. Accordingly, many Chinese manufacturers seem to prefer catering to this internal market behind protectionist barriers rather than venturing into the highly competitive and hence risky world of foreign exports. Moreover, inexperience with foreign trade, cumbersome bureaucratic red tape, low quality control of products, and an overvalued currency all handicap the PRC's export competitiveness. Nevertheless, China's recent adoption of a more outward-looking economic posture since the Cultural Revolution shows again that import substitution and export expansion are not mutually exclusive strategies of economic growth; they are more a matter of relative emphasis in the pursuit of this goal.

LAISSEZ-FAIRE VERSUS COMMAND ECONOMIES

Classical and neoclassical economists would attribute the economic successes of the capitalist East Asian countries to their deference to market forces. As we have seen, these scholars believe that the market provides the most efficient allocation of production factors, which results from the uncoordinated behavior of many individuals, each responding to the market's price signals. Classical and neoclassical economists therefore disapprove of governmental interventions in the marketplace because such interventions necessarily distort the price signals and result in a suboptimal allocation of production resources. In the view of Adam Smith, the eighteenth-century founder of classical economics, the activities of a government should be restricted to three roles: to protect society against a possible foreign invasion (by providing national defense), to protect citizens from each other (by providing law and order), and to create the necessary social and economic infrastructure (by providing public works and institutions). Classical economists believe that except for these limited functions, the government that governs least is the one that governs best.

In reality, the economic successes of the capitalist East Asian countries are a result of more than "just getting the price right." In particular, with the possible exception of Hong Kong, none of these countries practices the pure form of laissez-faire economics favored by the neo-classical economists (in a **laissez-faire economy,** the government allows the market to operate without any political interference and limits itself to the roles identified by Adam Smith). Indeed, even in Hong Kong, the British colonial government operates a very substantial enterprise in providing public housing to the residents. Moreover, to a substantial degree, Hong Kong's large banks have assumed some of the functions provided by governments elsewhere. For example, they coordinate their business decisions in order to ensure the financial stability and to stimulate the export competitiveness of the crown colony. Nevertheless, Hong Kong is a modern anachronism. As a colony living on borrowed land and on borrowed time, its days are quite literally numbered. The British have agreed to turn over its sovereignty to the PRC in 1997.

The opposite of a laissez-faire economy is a **command economy,** one in which the government allocates economic resources, stipulates production targets, and sets prices according to a master plan. The socialist countries typically have command economies. In these countries, the government instead of the market determines the levels of supply, demand, and price. The advocates of a planned, or command, economy argue that the assumptions of the classical and neoclassical economists are often unrealistic. For example, in the real world, competition among commercial suppliers is often low or nonexistent, serious production bottlenecks frequently afflict particular sectors, various production factors (e.g., capital, labor) have limited mobility, and the government has to step in to provide large industrial or transportation projects (airports, ports, communications facilities, energy plants) that are beyond the capacity of private entrepreneurs.

With the economic reforms that have been taking place in several socialist economies (the USSR, the PRC, Hungary, Poland), pure cases of a command economy have also become more rare. These reforms have given an increasing role to the market in lieu of the government's central plan in allocating resources and determining prices. They have also granted factory and farm managers more operational control and the workers more material incentives as a means of promoting greater productivity.

One scholar has described the PRC's economic system after the reforms of the 1980s as consisting of three mechanisms for influencing the supply and price of goods.[4] First, there is *mandatory planning*, whereby the government dictates production and price levels through administrative orders. Second, there is *guidance planning*, whereby the government employs a battery of indirect economic levers—such as credit subsidies, cheap raw materials, reduced taxes—to influence commodity output and price. Third, there is the *market mechanism*, whereby the government generally avoids intervention or only does so through the regulation of price.

Since the mid-1980s, the number of products subject to mandatory planning has fallen, whereas those belonging to the categories of guidance planning and market mechanism have risen. The former products are sold at fixed prices determined by the government, in contrast to the latter products, which do not have fixed prices. The latter products are allowed either to reflect market prices or to "float" (i.e., to fluctuate) within some range stipulated by the government.

This turn toward the market mechanism has brought substantial productivity growth in the Chinese cities as well as in the countryside. This growth, however, is not without some serious negative side effects: undesirable developments regarding price stability, job security, social equity, and political confidence. The latter developments provided fuel for the political turmoil and regime repression that became the focus of world media in the spring and summer of 1989 (a topic for Chapter 4).

More specifically, as one China scholar has put it,[5] the socioeconomic forces unleashed by Beijing's economic reforms threatened to upset the implicit social contract between state and society in the socialist countries. According to this interpretation, the people of these countries agree to give up some of the political and economic freedoms taken for granted in the West (employment freedom, competitive politics, independent press) in exchange for job security, income equality, and the provision of daily necessities and a social "safety net" (food, housing, education, medical care, old-age care) at low costs.

With the PRC's turn toward greater reliance on the market and less reliance on central planning, the government has withdrawn or reduced subsidies on many goods and services whose prices were previously kept artificially low. The resulting inflation for consumer goods, estimated to be running 20 percent and even 30 percent in 1989, created hardships for many families. The rising price of many goods made them inaccessible, since incomes of average Chinese workers (especially white-collar workers in the service sector, such as doctors, educators, civil servants) have lagged behind price increases. Concomitantly, workers in the private sector (street peddlers, food caterers, free-lance repair persons, farmers selling their produce on the free market) have prospered from the new economic freedoms encouraging personal entrepreneurship. The differences in incomes of Chinese citizens have become rather suddenly quite disturbingly large for a socialist country. In addition, with the new emphasis on worker productivity and job performance, managers have acquired greater autonomy in hiring—and firing—workers. Thus, the traditional values of social equity and job security have been compromised. Finally, as a result of the coexistence of two (fixed and unfixed) price systems, many officials have been tempted to cheat (by buying products from public enterprises at low fixed prices and reselling them at high nonfixed prices in the free market). Official corruption eroded public confidence and became yet another source of grievance that motivated the prodemocracy movement in the spring and summer of 1989.

In short, the recent Chinese experience shows that the transition from an economic system based on government planning to one that is more sensitive to market forces is neither unproblematic nor painless. It does carry a significant price tag in terms of economic stability and sociopolitical order. Consequently, categorical assertions regarding the merits of either laissez-faire or command economies are not likely to be very informative.

REGULATORY VERSUS DEVELOPMENTAL STATES

Most countries have a mixed economy, with elements of both government planning and market operation. Nevertheless, obviously there are variations of emphasis on these elements across different countries. Among the capitalist countries, the conceptual distinction between a **regulatory state,** one whose government refrains from interfering in the marketplace, except to ensure certain limited goals (e.g., antitrust regulations, protection of consumer rights) and a **developmental state,** one whose government intervenes actively in the economy in order to guide or promote particular substantive goals (e.g., full employment, export competitiveness, energy self-sufficiency) provides a useful basis for discussing the extent and nature of the government's role in economic affairs.[6]

For those countries that industrialized early (e.g., Britain and, to a lesser extent, the United States), the state (or government) has traditionally played a relatively restricted economic role. During the earlier years, their governments' economic activities dealt with such indispensable but limited functions as collecting taxes, issuing currency, and maintaining roads and ports. Subsequently, these governments expanded or deepened their involvement in areas such as regulating foreign trade, promoting commercial competition, and protecting consumers' rights. Thus, antitrust legislation and laws against commercial fraud came into being in order to ensure ethical business practices and the efficient operation of the market. The main objective of these regulatory activities is to enforce proper business forms and procedures or, as one scholar has put it,[7] to establish the rules of economic conduct. The government of a regulatory state does not want to make substantive decisions, such as which industries should be promoted for export or which imports should be discouraged through tariffs and quotas.

Countries that are late industrializers (e.g., Germany, Japan, the USSR) usually feature a more interventionist state. Their governments took a more active role in the initial industrialization drive, in part to offset the weaker entrepreneurial impulses in these countries and in part to promote and protect their domestic infant industries. Such official intervention in the economy took direct as well as indirect forms. Indirectly, easy credits, low taxes, secure and cheap supply of raw materials, guaranteed government purchases, and trade discrimination against foreign imports have been employed to help specific industries. Directly, the government could own, maintain, and operate various public enterprises (energy, steel, petrochemicals, shipbuilding, rail transportation) deemed essential for national defense or industrial development. In either case, a developmental state is concerned with the achievement of specific national goals such as export expansion, full employment, and security of energy supply. This emphasis on substantive, as opposed to procedural, goals distinguishes a developmental state from a regulatory state.

The U.S. government has historically been a regulatory state, although it has recently taken on some developmental activities. In contrast, Japan and the East Asian NICs tend to exemplify the developmental state. Indeed, in direct disagreement with the neoclassical scholars, who emphasize the role of the market and price in economic development, some scholars have attempted recently to explain the economic successes of the capitalist East Asian countries by focusing precisely on the role and strength of their respective states. This statist formulation argues that the capitalist East Asian countries have been able to achieve rapid and sustained economic ascendance because their governments have been strong and capable in nurturing and promoting those domestic industries that are internationally competitive, in marshaling resources for advantageous economic undertakings, in seeking out profitable niches in international markets and products, in regulating the economic and political influences of foreign companies, and in guiding the activities of the private sector and managing the demands from this sector. In short, instead of interpreting the East Asian economic achievements as evidence of the "magic of the marketplace," the statists see them as proof of the necessity of governmental guidance in industrial development.

In varying forms and to varying degrees, the most successful capitalist East Asian countries have developed powerful government agencies charged with the task of planning, guiding, and coordinating industrial policies. South Korea's Economic Planning Board, Taiwan's Council for Economic Planning and Development, and Singapore's Economic Development Board serve this vital function. However, the most well-known government institution of this kind, indeed, the one that served as the model for the South Koreans, Taiwanese, and Singaporeans, is Japan's Ministry of International Trade and Industry (MITI for short).

The bureaucrats of MITI have a very impressive array of policy tools at their disposal: the power to regulate foreign exchange, to screen foreign investment, and to license foreign technology. Through these administrative procedures, the Japanese government has in fact sought to "unbundle" the production package (discussed earlier in this chapter). The government has tried to secure the production ingredients that Japan either lacks or does not have in sufficient quantity or quality—specifically, foreign raw materials, external markets, and certain advanced technology from outside sources (such as in the aerospace and computer sectors). At the same time, it has discouraged other foreign inputs—specifically, foreign capital and management control—from entering Japan. In this sense, MITI has been called Japan's official doorman or gatekeeper. Its goal has been to foster national autonomy in vital industries such as steel, energy, computer, and telecommunication—or to put it in another way, to avoid foreign penetration and domination of these sensitive sectors. By welcoming some foreign inputs while barring others, MITI has tried to encourage specialization according to Japan's comparative advantage (as suggested by the neoclassical developmentalists) and, at the same time, to minimize that country's dependence on and therefore vulnerability to external suppliers (as advised by the dependency theorists).

MITI officials are also able to influence the availability and cost of bank loans, the relaxation of antitrust bans, the geographic location of particular plants, the supply of direct government subsidies, and the allocation of export quotas. Through these means, they have sought (sometimes successfully, sometimes not so successfully) to bring about mergers or collaboration among firms in order to reduce competition, limit production, and pool resources. They have also issued advisory directives (called "administrative guidance") that attempt to steer firms toward and to prepare them for tomorrow's "sunrise" industries (electronics, information systems) and, at the same time, to persuade them to shed yesterday's "sunset" industries (textiles, petrochemicals). In this way, Japanese firms are encouraged to move up the ladder of technology and pass the less desirable industries where Japanese competitiveness is declining (those with low technology content, high labor intensity, environmental pollution hazards) to follower nations such as Taiwan and South Korea. Given the heavy dependency of Japan's economy on exports, these steps are clearly designed to encourage continuous industrial adjustment and to stimulate dynamic trade competitiveness. Thus, in a sense, MITI—as Japan's official doorman—tries to control not only foreigners' access to the Japanese economy but also Japanese producers' access to foreign markets.[8]

The bureaucrats of MITI play a vital role in developing an industrial vision and in helping to realize this vision by encouraging cooperative behavior by consumers, producers, and elected officials. Whether owing to their political culture or tradition, these government officials have been generally able to avoid the penalties of fragmented interests and disjointed decision processes. Instead, MITI has been instrumental in facilitating information exchange and shared outlook between the Japanese public and private sectors. This close interaction and policy consensus have given rise to the image of "Japan, Inc." in the West.

By comparison, the U.S. regulatory state is more ponderous and fragmented. The various executive departments are often at odds with one another (not to mention the institutionalized tension between the executive and the legislative branches). At the same time, the decision processes of the United States also tend to be politicized and susceptible to the influence of particular vested interests. Thus, it seems that in the face of the Japanese "export machine" headed by MITI, the U.S. response to its deteriorating trade competitiveness has been rather inept and shortsighted.

More specifically, rising foreign shares of textiles, shoes, televisions, and automobiles in the U.S. market have been as much a political as an economic problem for Washington. The political problem stems from the lobbying efforts of domestic firms and labor unions that are faced with the prospect of profit and job losses as a result of foreign competition. Washington's response has been, in part, to institute protectionist measures: Called euphemistically **voluntary export restraints** (VERs) and **orderly marketing agreements** (OMAs), these are bilateral agreements negotiated with selected foreign producers to restrict the quantity of certain imports. These restrictions result in what economists call **scarcity rent**—the profits that are accrued by producers when a shortage of supply drives up prices. These increased prices paid by consumers provide a temporary relief to domestic producers. Yet this temporary relief is often insufficient to motivate them to become more efficient and competitive.

The foreign producers can share the benefits of scarcity rent. They are also apt to "move upscale"—that is, to push into the more dynamic and expensive end of the market. Thus, for example, previous U.S. trade restrictions against Taiwanese and South Korean cotton fabrics had the effect of encouraging the East Asian producers to move to synthetic fibers. Similarly, the quantitative limit placed on the import of Japanese automobiles (2.3 million in 1989) has motivated Toyota, Nissan, and Honda to export the more expensive models (and to load them with all sorts of options) in an attempt to compensate for the lower sales volume by increasing the profit margins. Thus, the impact of quantitative trade restrictions imposed by the United States is softened and deflected by the East Asian exporters through qualitative product upgrading.[9] Because the profits of these exporters can be maintained and even increased under VERs and OMAs, they are often quite happy to continue to comply with the quantitative restrictions even after the import quotas have expired.

U.S. import restrictions have also encouraged foreigners to bring their plants to North America (the United States, Canada, and Mexico) in order to bypass these trade barriers. This development has been particularly noticeable in the automobile industry, as the major Japanese producers have all started to manufacture cars in the United States. Foreign investment in U.S. production facilities naturally creates jobs for U.S. workers and thus is politically appealing to politicians (who can boast of "bringing home the bacon"). However, it also puts an increasing portion of domestic production capacity under foreign ownership and management control—a situation that, as we have seen, Japan's MITI has sought strenuously to avoid. According to one estimate,[10] by the early 1990s Japanese firms will control 40 to 45 percent of all cars sold in the United States—not counting Japanese cars imported by General Motors and Chrysler under U.S. license.

It seems that import restrictions may therefore only in the short run help to contain the danger of corporate bankruptcy and worker unemployment, developments that would of course have an adverse effect on social order and political popularity. These measures address, however, the symptoms and not the causes of deteriorating trade competitiveness. Indeed, they may have the perverse effect of postponing the necessary (and painful) steps of industrial adjustment facing domestic producers, while prompting foreign producers to innovate and diversify their products. Thus, in the long run, import restrictions may work more to the advantage of the latter than the former. In the absence of an official "gatekeeper," the consequent inflow of foreign capital may also undermine national autonomy.

In the final analysis, the export competitiveness of the capitalist East Asian countries reflects not only the policies of their governments but also—and more important—the commercial adaptability of their manufacturers and entrepreneurs. Although these countries at one time had a comparative advantage in relatively cheap labor costs, that is no longer true. Countries with even lower labor costs (the Philippines, Thailand, and the PRC) have joined the game of export expansion. Instead, an important asset of Japanese firms has been their flexible specialization rather than cost minimization based on "Fordism" (large-scale assembly-line production of standardized manufactures that attempts to capture economies of scale, a method that was first introduced by the Ford Motor Company). This flexibility in manufacturing and export promotion enables Japanese firms to adjust constantly to the changing international market.[11] Similarly, Hong Kong, Singapore, Taiwan, and South Korea have been more successful than the Latin American countries in expanding their manufactured exports because the former have shown a greater adaptability to market conditions. Quite apart from competitive pricing, the East Asians have paid more attention to matters such as changing consumer tastes, design innovation, product upgrading, quality control, and prompt delivery.[12] Import quotas or tariffs do not foster these competitive assets. VERs and OMAs are likely instead to induce a sense of complacency among domestic producers who can hide behind protectionist barriers and reap the benefits of scarcity rent.

The preceding remarks in turn suggest that the oft-heard charges of "unfair trade" made by U.S. officials and manufacturers against the East Asian exporters do not reveal the full reason for the mounting U.S. trade deficit. Although the East Asians do engage in a variety of discriminatory trade practices, their commercial protectionism is no more extensive than that of the Latin Americans or even the West Europeans. In fact, formal and informal barriers against foreign imports have been dismantled at a more rapid pace in East Asia than in Latin America and Western Europe. The inability of U.S. manufacturers to penetrate the East Asian markets is historically linked with the inward-looking orientation of most of them. That is, given the huge size of the domestic consumer market, U.S. producers have had little incentive to focus on foreign sales. In contrast, limited domestic demand has forced the East Asian manufacturers to pay particular attention to the changing needs and tastes of foreign customers. This disparity in relative attention to external market conditions accounts for the differences in commercial adaptability and flexibility on the part of the manufacturers on opposite sides of the Pacific Ocean.[13] It also explains why Japanese products sell much better than U.S. products in Taiwan, South Korea, and Southeast Asia (if the latter countries practiced systematic discrimination against foreign goods, Japanese and U.S. products would do equally poorly).

LABOR, LANDLORDS, AND FOREIGN FIRMS

The policy capacity and policy conduct of a government are influenced by and embedded in the historical and institutional context. Thus, whether a country develops a regulatory or developmentalist state and whether its government pursues import substitution or export expansion result from the interplay of several important historical factors, as reflected in the following questions: How strong is the country's labor movement, and have the workers been included in or excluded from the ruling coalition? How dependent has the country been in the past on the export of cash crops (e.g., cotton, tobacco, sugar), and have rural conservative interests been able to shape its developmental course? When did foreign multinational corporations arrive in the country, and what has been the extent of their involvement in the local economy? Did they invest in agriculture, mining, or manufacturing operations? The answers to these questions help to explain the different developmental histories of countries.

One of the hallmarks of the capitalist East Asian economies has been the political subjugation of their industrial workers. In these countries the industrial labor force is heavily regulated and controlled by the government. Union organization was banned in some countries except under official auspices, and industrial strikes have been ruthlessly suppressed by the riot police. The weakness of organized labor in these countries results in turn in low levels of governmental provision for social welfare. In a variety of areas—such as unemployment benefits, maternity leaves, minimum wage laws, compensation for industrial accidents, regulation of occupational safety standards, and old-age pension funds—the East Asian workers fare much worse than their North American and, indeed, their Latin American counterparts.

The political weakness and docility of capitalist East Asia's industrial work force can, of course, be traced to the civil wars or foreign occupation in Japan, China, and Korea in the aftermath of World War II. The perceived threat from the political Left led to a crackdown on organized labor by right-wing regimes, aided by Washington. Thus, the industrial workers of Japan, South Korea, and Taiwan have been kept out of their country's ruling coalitions, which have been composed of big business, conservative politicians, and powerful bureaucrats. In Singapore labor representatives have been effectively co-opted by the ruling People's Action Party, whereas in Hong Kong waves of refugees from the PRC have kept wages low and worker consciousness weak.

The disorganization of industrial workers in capitalist East Asia has also sprung from its paternalistic system of employment. In Japan, for example, industrial workers are typically assured lifetime employment and are paid wages according to their seniority. Year-end bonuses for workers provide a form of profit sharing in the company's commercial successes. These features tend to promote a strong sense of worker identification with the company and a willingness to collaborate with the management. In contrast, labor and management often treat each other as adversaries in the United States. Moreover, unlike Japanese workers, who can expect lifetime employment, U.S. workers tend to see the introduction of new technologies as a source of threat to their job security.

The political weakness and docility of industrial workers in the capitalist East Asian countries made possible the development of strong states under the stewardship of authoritarian and developmentally oriented bureaucrats, as we have seen. These strong states were in turn able to apply various administrative levers for the purpose of stimulating and promoting timely industrial adjustments. Thus, the capitalist East Asian countries have been better able to weather repeated economic shocks (such as the energy crises, U.S. protectionism, global recessions) than their North American, European, and Latin American counterparts. Unencumbered by strong labor movements, their conservative, business-oriented ruling coalitions have been able to pass on the costs of industrial adjustment to the workers. In particular, the employees of the smaller and less efficient enterprises in these countries serve as "shock absorbers" in times of economic hardship.

In contrast, strong labor movements in the Western countries and their long-standing participation as part of ruling coalitions mean that the interests of workers must be taken into account in attempting any industrial adjustment. By the same token, the governments of Western countries are more open and susceptible to lobbying by organized labor. Thus, for example, our discussion in the previous section suggested that the U.S. government has been under great pressure to adopt protectionist measures for the purpose of saving and creating domestic jobs. As another example, the governments of Mexico and Argentina—both subject to the influence of strong and institutionalized labor interests—traditionally have had great difficulty in enforcing austerity programs that require depressing industrial wages and raising commodity prices. In short, these political economies are less "governable" in part because their states are less powerful and autonomous than those of the East Asians.

A docile work force and low social overhead (low levels of provision for social welfare) have constituted the foundation of the export-led growth strategy of the capitalist East Asian countries. As we have seen, this strategy was initially applied to the manufacture and export of labor-intensive products. Since the 1960s, the East Asian NICs (though not Japan) have also solicited foreign capital and technology in an attempt to consolidate their positions as export platforms. Many foreign firms have been attracted to them precisely because of their malleable labor force and probusiness climate.

Naturally, dependency theorists would argue that foreign investment often brings in its wake undesirable consequences, such as distorted economic growth, widening social inequality, and declining national autonomy.[14] Large multinational corporations (MNCs) have in the past achieved a dominant economic and political influence in some Third World countries (e.g., Firestone in Liberia, Aramco in Saudi Arabia, Anaconda and Kennecott in Chile, and United Fruit in Central America). Indeed, these companies were sometimes more powerful than their host governments, thus undermining the latter's political autonomy. The penetration of foreign economic interests has also led to a process of "denationalization" whereby an increasing portion of domestic means of production falls into foreign ownership or management control.

Fortunately for the capitalist East Asian NICs, the MNCs did not view them as attractive investment sites in the 1950s. The political and military tension in their region (due primarily to the lingering effects of the Chinese and Korean civil wars) made foreign investment a risky proposition at that time. Moreover, unlike some Latin American and African countries, Taiwan, South Korea, Hong Kong, and Singapore had neither large domestic markets nor abundant natural resources to offer the MNCs. The MNCs did not become interested in the latter countries until the 1960s—primarily because of their relatively skilled and inexpensive labor force, a comparative advantage that made them attractive as export platforms for consumer goods and light-industrial products. However, by that time, the native entrepreneurs and industrialists had already acquired sufficient expertise, capital, and market share to resist foreign competition and takeover. Therefore, the process of denationalization did not take place in the East Asian NICs in the way that it so frequently occurred in other parts of the Third World.

This is not to say that foreign capital has not dominated selected sectors of the capitalist East Asian economies. It has, for example, in Taiwan's electronics industry and Singapore's petrochemical industry. However, these foreign-dominated sectors have not competed with local businesses (in any case, the domestic markets of the East Asian NICs are too small to absorb their products) but instead have been geared to export their products to overseas markets. The MNCs (mostly owned and operated by Americans and Japanese) and the East Asian NICs have a symbiotic relationship, with the former contributing capital and technology and the latter contributing land and labor. In this partnership, the MNCs reap the export profits, whereas the host countries benefit from the creation of jobs and the transfer of technology and market know-how.

In the case just described, the MNCs are recruited to establish an industry (e.g., electronics, information-processing systems, petrochemicals) that a developing country—because of its lack of the necessary capital and technology—would be unable to launch on its own. It is quite different from the situation described previously regarding the U.S. automobile industry, where domestic production has long existed but is being increasingly "squeezed" by newer foreign-owned facilities.

Foreign investments in East Asia's "four little tigers" have been almost exclusively in the manufacturing sector. This is another factor that sets their experience apart from those of the Latin American, African, and Southeast Asian countries. In the latter countries, foreign investments have historically gone to agricultural production and mineral extraction, such as sugar in the Philippines, rubber and tin in Malaya, and petroleum in Indonesia. It is significant that foreign investments in these latter areas tend to foster vested social and economic interests opposed to industrial modernization. Furthermore, compared to the MNCs' manufacturing operations, the technological and industrial spin-off effects of investments in the production of primary goods are very limited.

This discussion has brought us back to the notion of a strong state that regulates the level and nature of foreign penetration of a domestic economy. As already discussed, the Japanese government has played an important gatekeeping role in this regard. The Taiwanese and, to a lesser extent, the Singaporean governments have also performed this role.[15] They have designated priority industries (usually in the advanced technological sectors) where foreign investments would be given special preferential treatment. They have, moreover, discouraged foreign investment or ownership in areas where there is already a surplus production capacity, where they want to protect their domestic infant industries, or where a sensitive issue of national security is involved. To ensure the benefits of foreign investment and to avoid its harmful effects, the

Taiwanese government also stipulates that the MNCs must purchase a minimum amount of local inputs (the "domestic-contents requirement") and export a minimum amount of its finished products. Taipei also sets guidelines on the amount of profits that can be repatriated (returned to the home country of the MNC) and the kind of inputs (equipment, raw materials) that can be imported for the MNC's operation on the island. The South Korean government has at its disposal similar administrative tools, although it has historically preferred to seek foreign loans rather than direct investment.

Given their small size, Hong Kong and Singapore never had any agricultural or mining potential to attract foreign interest. In contrast, Taiwan and South Korea were once Japan's colonies and had provided significant amounts of rice, sugar, and minerals to that country. The Japanese defeat in World War II, however, removed one major impediment to their eventual graduation from the role of exporters of primary goods. The Chinese and Korean civil wars also left important legacies for the subsequent industrialization of those countries. As discussed in Chapter 2, the Taiwanese and South Korean elites, detached from their traditional power base in mainland China and northern Korea, were finally in the 1950s able and willing to undertake meaningful land reforms. These reforms were economically important because they helped to stimulate increased agricultural productivity, and the rural surpluses in turn helped to promote industrial growth. The reforms were also politically important because they undercut the power of the landlord class, thereby eliminating one possible source of challenge to the emergent developmental state. The brief occupation of South Korea by the North Korean forces during the civil war also helped this process, as the Communist land reforms virtually decimated the landlord class in some locales.

As did a docile labor force, a politically subdued landlord class facilitated the rise of a strong developmental state in Taiwan and South Korea. These countries do not have an entrenched rural elite that might have opposed indigenous industrialization. In the Latin American countries with important agricultural exports (e.g., beef and wheat in Argentina, coffee in Colombia, bananas in Honduras, and sugar in Cuba), the plantation owners and trade merchants have traditionally favored the continued specialization in these primary products as well as the import of foreign manufactured goods. They have usually objected to import-substitution policies because such policies would reallocate economic resources to the detriment of their export interests. To a significant extent, the voice of such rural oligarchs and a comprador class was not raised in Taiwan's and South Korea's industrialization effort. In contrast, the owners of sugar and rubber plantations have enjoyed a more entrenched and dominant position in the political economies of the

Philippines and Malaysia respectively. Consequently, the states of these two Southeast Asian countries have been less strong and autonomous and their industrialization attempts more halting and checkered in comparison with those of Taiwan and South Korea.

In summary, the economic successes of Japan, Taiwan, South Korea, and Singapore seem to have been helped by their respective developmental states. The strength, autonomy, and policy capacity of the developmental state of each have been the result of several historical legacies that have enabled the capitalist East Asian countries to keep labor demands down, foreign domination out, and rural oligarchs subdued.[16] These conditions, in turn, have increased their capacity for market adaptability and industrial upgrading. Conversely, the absence of these conditions in the Philippines and in Latin America has resulted in their political incapacity to undertake coherent, sustained, and effective policies of economic adjustment.

BETWEEN POWER AND WEALTH: JAPANESE AND U.S. SECURITY PRACTICES

During the 1950s and 1960s, Washington was much more concerned with the pursuit of power than of wealth. Endowed with the world's largest economy, most advanced technologies, and abundant natural resources, Americans took their national wealth for granted. The only plausible challenger to U.S. power in the world was the USSR, and the threat posed by Moscow was decidedly military and ideological rather than economic in nature. Thus, it seemed quite natural for Washington to define national security primarily in terms of the military containment of and ideological competition with communism.

Accordingly, U.S. officials paid far more attention to international politics than to international economics, and international politics was perceived almost exclusively in terms of the rivalry between the two superpowers. In this rivalry, each side tried to recruit as many allies as possible (in the case of the United States, the North Atlantic Treaty Organization and the Southeast Asia Treaty Organization are prominent examples). The consequent U.S. worldview was highly dichotomous, assigning countries to either "our" side or "their" side. This worldview implied that a geographic demarcation could somehow be clearly drawn between the two sides and that transgressions by the other side across this line constituted clear evidence of aggression that had to be turned back. This reasoning, of course, underlay Washington's *containment policy* against communism.

At the time, the bilateral contest between capitalism and communism was seen by U.S. officials as a zero-sum game in the sense that any gain by one side necessarily meant a loss for the other side. And the gains and losses were in turn defined primarily in territorial terms (e.g., the "loss" of China, North Korea, and South Vietnam), even though there existed also an awareness of and concern with psychological consequences (e.g., the ostensible demoralizing chain reaction that defeat in one country would cause in other countries, a concern that gave rise to the "domino theory"). This reasoning again tended to reinforce static geographic definitions of national security and interest, such as those expressed in traditional notions of a great power's spheres of influence and its capability to project military influence abroad.

Typically, U.S. perceptions and evaluations of the balance of forces between it and the USSR also reflected a primary concern with tangible military capabilities, such as the number of bombs, tanks, and divisions commanded by each side. Similarly, the primary instruments for contesting political power and managing international crises were military in nature. Wars had to be deterred and communism contained through the visible and credible display and, if need be, use of armed forces. The doctrines of massive retaliation, flexible response, and anti-insurgency warfare all stemmed from this belief in the efficacy of military instrumentation. This belief also meant that Washington tended to "oversubscribe" military security; that is, the United States was inclined to pay more for defense than other countries, to continue weapons purchases after achieving a capability for the assured destruction of its adversaries, and to adopt a geographically and ideologically extensive view of national security (e.g., "making the world safe for democracy," extensive alliance networks to contain communism in Asia and Europe).

In short, traditional U.S. thinking tended to treat national security almost exclusively in terms of superpower competition that was delineated according to alliance and territorial boundaries and evaluated according to military capabilities and instruments. In a sense, these characteristics also applied to Tokyo's strategic thinking in the 1930s and 1940s, when Japan launched a campaign of military conquest to establish its regional hegemony. Called the "Greater East Asian Co-Prosperity Sphere" by Tokyo's propagandists, this Japanese attempt at asserting physical control over foreign markets, resources, and populations turned out to be an utter disaster. Japan was decisively defeated in World War II and was physically occupied by the victorious U.S. forces.

In contrast to the traditional U.S. security approach, the Japanese have in the recent years put forth the idea of **comprehensive national security,** which combines military with political and economic concerns. These concerns range from the strengthening of Tokyo's Self-Defense Forces to the fostering of friendly relations with its neighbors. Particular emphasis is given also to the stabilization of Japan's external trade relations and the search for secure sources of foreign raw materials. The Japanese doctrine of comprehensive national security avoids overt military means of guaranteeing security and relies instead primarily on economic statecraft.

Given the heavy dependency of Japan's economy on foreign markets and supplies of energy and foodstuffs, it is small wonder that Tokyo is especially concerned with securing commercial access to foreign markets and supplies. Disruption of this access poses a far more probable danger to Japan's national security than an overt military attack on its home islands. Tokyo is especially keen to assure a stable supply of foreign energy, which constitutes the lifeline of the Japanese economy. To achieve this goal, it tries to diversify its suppliers (hence, to avoid overreliance on any one source) and to nurture incentives on the part of these suppliers that favor continued provision of oil to Japan (such as by making these countries dependent on Japanese investment and technology). At the same time, it engages in the stockpiling of strategic reserves, development of alternative energy sources and technologies (coal, nuclear), and coordination with other oil importers in order to dampen the shock of any possible supply interruption.[17] Finally, the Japanese government and energy industry stress the security of their energy supply far more than the monetary cost of this supply; they customarily import foreign energy at prices that are higher than the prevailing international norm. Whereas Americans seem usually prepared to overpay for their military superiority and to pursue a surplus security in this area, the Japanese have instead been more inclined to pay a premium to ensure extra reliability in the foreign supply of their energy needs.[18]

In addition to foreign commerce, Japan's pursuit of comprehensive national security has increasingly relied on foreign investment and assistance. As we have seen, Japan's foreign investment has been used to foster close commercial and political ties with strategically located allies (those situated at choke points on the sea-lanes that connect Japan with its trade partners) and vital suppliers of raw materials. Japan's trade partners, to the extent that they are dependent on its continued provision of capital and technology, have a vested interest in not disrupting the ongoing relationship.

Since the 1980s, the role of investment has been increasingly complemented by that of aid. Japan has become the world's largest donor of foreign assistance. Its aid program also stresses the promotion of cordial relations with those countries that are important to Japanese businesses as either customers or suppliers (such as the PRC, which offers a huge market for Japanese products, and Indonesia, which supplies Japanese industries with petroleum). Alternatively, Japanese aid dollars are allocated to countries—for example, Thailand, the Philippines, Malaysia, Burma, South Korea, Pakistan, and Egypt—that are strategically important to Japan's formal or tacit regional allies (namely, the United States and the PRC). To a significant extent, Japanese developmental aid reinforces Washington's and Beijing's military assistance to foster friendly regimes in countries that are close to areas of ongoing or possible armed conflict (e.g., Cambodia, Afghanistan, Iran-Iraq, Israel). The primary targets of Japanese economic aid have been the Asian countries, with the PRC and several members of the Association of Southeast Asian Nations (specifically, Indonesia, Thailand, the Philippines, and Malaysia) leading the pack.

The Japanese have, of course, made much of their supposed "military allergy" and "nuclear aversion" derived from their disastrous defeat in World War II. According to this view, Japanese public opinion would object to high defense expenditures and would certainly oppose any projection of Japanese military influence abroad. In contrast, U.S. officials and scholars have in the recent past repeatedly emphasized the theme that Japan has not paid a fair share of the costs of collective defense. They charge that Tokyo has been a **free rider** (a country or person that benefits from a public good that it has not adequately paid for), hitching itself to the military coattails of the United States. Some even argue that Japan's economic successes have been the result of its low defense spending, made possible by the protective shield offered by the U.S. conventional forces stationed in and around Japan and by the U.S. nuclear umbrella.

Neither of those images is entirely accurate. As already mentioned, Japan does contribute to the collective security of Western countries through the application of nonmilitary instruments. It cannot be denied that Japanese capital, technology, and especially developmental assistance fulfill a strategic purpose.[19] Indeed, in a very important way, they pick up the slack and fill the gaps when and where U.S. military projection would be unwise or infeasible. Thus, Tokyo's foreign economic and commercial policies often pursue a track complementary to Washington's political and military measures.

It would also be quite misleading to suggest that Japan is a powerless giant, an economic behemoth without any military capabilities. This suggestion evidently suits Tokyo's publicists, who want to foster a pacific image of their country abroad, an image that would help to deflect foreign adversaries from focusing on Japan as a potential military target and to defuse concerns on the part of Japan's neighbors that somehow it could repeat its military aggression of World War II. However, in reality, Japan is far from being militarily impotent. It has the world's third largest defense budget (behind only the United States and the

USSR). Furthermore, given Japan's large industrial base and sophisticated technological establishment, it could launch a massive and effective military armament program on short notice. This program, should Tokyo choose to undertake it, could easily put Japan in the role of a military balance tipper in the competition between the United States and the USSR.

The superpowers as well as Japan's other neighbors (especially the PRC and Korea) would most likely be worse rather than better off if Japan were to remilitarize fully. That is, their security situation is more likely to deteriorate than to improve should Japan develop the full array of capabilities for military assertion abroad. Compared to such a scenario, letting Japan be a free rider looks much more attractive. Stated more baldly, if the United States is already having so much trouble coping with the Japanese economic challenge, how would it like to contend with a militarily revitalized Japan that could seriously challenge Washington's interests and influence in the Pacific region, as it did once during World War II?

Being quite aware of this concern of not only U.S. but also Soviet and Chinese generals and military planners, Tokyo exploits it skillfully to its own advantage. By appealing to the self-interest of foreigners who would be better off in a world without a militarized Japan, Tokyo hopes to lessen external pressure to increase its defense spending further and to deter foreign threats of market closure and supply stoppage. This is certainly a very different approach to national security from that of the United States, with its traditional concern about and reliance on military capability and assertion.

CONCLUSION

Various kinds of policy conduct and historical contexts pertaining to the pursuit of growth, order, and security in East Asia have been discussed in this chapter. The export-oriented economic expansion of the capitalist countries in this region has been stressed in scholarly as well as official circles. Yet it should be remembered that this economic success has had its costs—especially in terms of the suppression of organized labor, the low levels of public support for social welfare, the rule of authoritarian politicians and bureaucrats with little public accountability, the heavy dependence on foreign markets and supplies as engines of domestic growth, and the political-ideological conformity with and deference to Washington in its competition with Moscow. We can ask whether this is a reasonable price tag for rapid economic growth.

We need to recognize that the strategies adopted by the East Asian trading nations are not likely to be successfully replicated elsewhere.

These strategies have "paid off" in part because of conducive historical legacies and lucky timing—such as the massive U.S. aid during the 1950s, a prosperous global economy during the 1960s, and the guiding hand of a strong developmental state. However, rapid socioeconomic change is undermining the very conditions that had facilitated the earlier export-led growth in capitalist East Asia. Opposition parties are emerging in Taiwan and South Korea, and voices demanding political liberalization are being heard. Organized labor is becoming stronger, and the salaries for skilled workers have gone up tremendously since the demand for their services has increased faster than the supply. Additionally, various interest groups are demanding greater government support for social welfare, protection of consumer rights, and commitment to environmental preservation. Thus, the developmental states of capitalist East Asia have become less dominant in their relations with social groups—an outcome brought about by the success of their economic strategy.

At the same time, the capitalist East Asian trading nations are increasingly being squeezed abroad. On the one hand, their export successes have raised concerns about balance of payment and lost jobs among their trade partners. As we have seen, demands for protectionism have increased in the United States. On the other hand, other countries have begun to imitate the capitalist East Asians. The Philippines, Thailand, and the PRC can boast of even lower wages as a means of luring foreign investors and expanding their market shares abroad. That is to say, the comparative advantage of an inexpensive labor pool is shifting away from South Korea, Taiwan, Singapore, and Hong Kong—which are in turn forced to seek new market niches. Taiwan and South Korea in particular have been upgrading their industrial structure and attempting to move into the more capital- and knowledge-intensive sectors of consumer durables (automobiles, household appliances, personal computers). This development, however, will in turn put pressure on Japanese exporters. Therefore, instead of an orderly formation of the flying geese pattern, the sunrise industries of a later generation of industrializing countries may bump into the sunset industries of an earlier generation of industrialized countries (e.g., Chinese textile exports challenging the Hong Kong and Taiwanese textile manufacturers, South Korean exports of steel and automobiles cutting into Japan's market share). As a result, industrial competition and export rivalry could very well intensify in the near future.

FOUR

□ □ □

Virtuous Cycle or Deleterious Feedback?

$\boxed{E}$ver since the end of World War II, the political economy of the Third World has been a matter of ongoing concern and interest in Western scholarly and official circles. During the 1950s and the 1960s, a certain air of confidence and optimism prevailed. Western scholars and officials alike held up the historical experiences of their own countries (especially those of Britain and the United States) as a universal model for replication elsewhere. It was believed that Third World countries would basically have to go through the same stages of development experienced by their Western predecessors; and if they followed the lessons of the latter's development, they would also be successful. Consequently, there was quite a bit of ethnocentrism in analytic as well as policy treatments of the Third World's modernization, a process that was in the minds of many people the same thing as Westernization.

What are the so-called lessons to be derived from the developmental experiences of the Western world—especially those of Britain and the United States? First, it was supposed that "development" entailed the replacement of traditional values and outlooks by modern ones: for example, individual initiative, achievement-oriented personality, commercial entrepreneurship, Protestant work ethic, and social incentives to save and invest. These were essential stimuli for economic growth and social mobility. Second, many observers emphasized the role of capitalism and market competition as important ingredients in the industrialization of Britain and the United States. There was therefore a strong belief in the "magic of the marketplace," and a concomitant disdain for governmental intervention in the economy. Third, it was presumed that economic development would accompany social and political development defined in terms of open mobility channels and pluralistic, competitive politics. Social mobility and pluralistic politics would unleash the creative forces for business entrepreneurship and industrial growth, whereas economic progress would in turn facilitate and promote social stability and liberal democracy. Finally, some analysts asserted a connection between a country's socioeconomic underdevelopment and its susceptibility to domestic insurrection and foreign aggression. According to this view, the United States should help in the promotion of Western values and institutions as well as in the eradication of poverty in Third World countries such as South Vietnam in order to counter the threat of Communist insurgency and infiltration.

The above summary presents a rather rosy Western view of the Third World's developmental prospects, a view that was quite widely shared during the 1950s and 1960s. It suggests not only that the Third World countries could follow the footsteps of the Western countries in their modernization attempts but also that the various policy values tend to reinforce and stimulate each other. Somehow, good things—economic growth, market competition, social mobility, liberal democracy, internal stability, and external security—were seen as going together. After all, did not the developmental histories of Britain and the United States produce all these felicitous outcomes? There was therefore supposed to be a *virtuous cycle* of modernization.

Alas, this optimistic view did not last very long. Even during the 1960s, contrary evidence began to accumulate. It seemed that the various policy values just mentioned did not interact in a linear, straightforward, or synergistic manner. Instead, their interactions suggested the possible existence of *deleterious feedback*. Thus, for instance, rapid economic growth was found to increase political instability, exacerbate income inequality, undermine the prospects for establishing liberal democratic institutions, and intensify international tension and conflict. Similarly, social stability, competitive politics, and long-standing peace could have an adverse effect on a country's economic growth and income equality. These findings reminded officials and scholars alike that they should seriously consider possible *trade-offs* in the pursuit of various policy desiderata.

In this chapter I discuss the accomplishments and failures of selective countries in the Pacific Basin in light of this tension among alternative policy goals. The developmental histories of the East Asian countries feature some surprises as well as ironies. Thus, for example, Taiwan, South Korea, Hong Kong, and Singapore have been able to sustain rapid economic growth and, at the same time, maintain relatively high levels of income equality and political stability (values that, according to cross-national research, tend to undermine rather than reinforce each other).

As another example, although these countries and Japan had all suffered military defeat and foreign occupation in their recent history, they were able to recover from their wartime devastation and achieve economic performances superior to those of the victorious countries (the United States, Britain, Australia in World War II). And even though organized labor has been traditionally suppressed in capitalist East Asia (see Chapter 3), there is greater income equality and higher physical quality of life in that region than in capitalist Latin America (where organized labor has traditionally enjoyed more political influence).

Finally, although in the 1950s and 1960s many scholars perceived Confucianism as the embodiment of traditional values and as such an obstacle to modernization, the recent economic success of the capitalist East Asian countries has led to an analytic reversal. Traditional Chinese culture is now said to impart attitudes—such as a strong work ethic, a reverence for authority and stability, an emphasis on the values of education and family, and a willingness to subordinate individual preferences to group norms—conducive to modern economic undertakings. The persistence of these traditional values, rather than the adoption of Western orientations, is used by some analysts to explain the economic success of countries (Taiwan, Korea, Japan, Singapore, Hong Kong) influenced by traditional Chinese culture.[1]

Accordingly, the recent developmental histories of the East Asian countries feature prominent puzzles, paradoxes, and even contradictions that challenge prevailing Western scholarly theories and conventional wisdom. We turn to explore and discuss some of these apparent enigmas.

RAPID GROWTH
AND POLITICAL INSTABILITY

Many people believe that economic development goes hand in hand with political stability and liberal democracy and that poverty and social deprivation are a sure recipe for political instability, rebellion, and repression. To a substantial degree, this belief is valid. Cross-national research has consistently shown that countries with high levels of income and industrialization tend to be more stable and more democratic than those with low levels. The well-to-do countries have a much better chance than the poorer ones of developing and sustaining stable democratic institutions.[2]

Why? Increasing wealth and industrialization tend to raise the income of workers and to expand the size of the middle class, thereby giving more people a stake in the existing socioeconomic order. Economic development is accompanied by rising education level, which in turn is related to greater tolerance for political diversity and commitment to democratic values in the population. Finally, economic development usually takes place in the context of increasing urbanization and modern communication (newspapers, radio, television), which provide the necessary general environment for nurturing democratic ethos and institutions.

The above effects of the *level* of economic development on political stability and liberal democracy, however, should be clearly distinguished from the influence of the *rate* of economic growth. The latter concept refers to the speed of a country's economic growth (i.e., how fast it occurs). Generally speaking, the faster this growth, the greater will be the danger of political instability and repression. There exists therefore an important trade-off relationship between the pursuit of rapid economic growth on the one hand and the preservation of political stability and liberalization on the other.

What are the reasons for this trade-off relationship? It must be remembered that economic development is an inherently traumatic process that involves the destruction of an existing socioeconomic order and its replacement by a new one. In this process, many traditional skills and jobs become obsolete. Unemployment and underemployment can be quite high because many workers are not suitable for employment in modern enterprises. At the same time, inflation tends to diminish the income of those who are employed. The prices of daily necessities usually rise much faster than wages; thus many goods become unaffordable for ordinary consumers. For the above reasons, rapid economic growth is apt to increase rather than decrease the gap between the rich and the poor. According to one economist, during periods of rapid economic growth, a country's "median income might fall while average income rises."[3] That is to say, the fruits of economic growth are distributed unequally, so that a small minority tends to profit from it far more than the rest of society.

Naturally, economic growth redistributes not only income but also social prestige and political power. For instance, the plantation owners of Latin America and the religious clerics of Iran would have their traditional positions undermined rather than enhanced as a result of the social changes brought about by rapid economic growth. They would become less influential than modern industrialists and secular opinion leaders. Similarly, the economic standing and social status of bazaar merchants, moneylenders, and traditional scholars would be threatened by the introduction of Western-style supermarkets, banking institutions, and education systems. Thus, rapid economic growth produces many social as well as financial "losers" and a smaller number of "winners."

Even when the average level of social and economic well-being of a country is improving rapidly, many people will still feel frustrated. They compare how well they are doing with how well their peers are doing. Someone whose income has gone up from $50 to $70 is apt to be displeased rather than pleased if his neighbor's income has risen from $40 to $100. The first person feels that he is losing ground relative to his neighbor—a phenomenon known as **relative deprivation.**[4] Relative deprivation refers to a sense of grievance based on the perceived gap between one's present socioeconomic standing and one's aspirations for this standing. The greater this gap, the greater will be this sense of grievance—and, hence, the greater will be the danger of social rebellion and political disorder.

It is important to note that according to the theory of relative deprivation, social and political stability is *not* a direct function of the absolute level of poverty or deprivation in a society. Many poor countries in Africa are quite stable. Instead, the key determinant of stability is the *difference* between one's current socioeconomic conditions and one's hopes for a better life. When hopes are low or nonexistent, people do not protest against their lot; they instead accept passively their "fate." However, when people believe that they deserve a better life and that this better life is possible, they become politically active. Thus, political protest and instability are likely to stem from the *revolution of rising expectations*—that is, when people's expectations for a better life rise faster than the actual improvements in their life.

Where do people derive their expectations? These expectations are a direct result of the processes—education, urbanization, and communications—that accompany economic development. As people become better educated, live in urban communities, and learn about life elsewhere (through Hollywood movies, visits to the United States), they come to expect more from life. Conversely, when people are illiterate, live in isolated rural communities, and have no idea about the possibilities of improving their life, they do not rebel—even though, by objective standards, their living conditions are appalling. Accordingly, the rapidly changing middle-income countries (as opposed to the really backward societies) are more likely to experience political instability. Political protest and governmental repression often follow or accompany rapid economic growth, such as in Iran in the late 1970s.

People also form expectations of a better life as a result of governmental reforms, which give people the hope for further improvements. In the words of the astute French political observer de Tocqueville two centuries ago, "the social order destroyed by a revolution is almost always better than that which immediately preceded it, and experience shows that the most dangerous moment for a bad government is generally that in which it sets about reform."[5] Indeed, the American, French, and Russian revolutions took place, not during the darkest days of regime repression, but actually when the authorities were taking steps to improve conditions. Similarly and more recently, the shah of Iran, Ferdinand Marcos of the Philippines, and several Communist leaders of Eastern Europe did try to introduce some reform—even though these changes were too little and too late to prevent their overthrow. Thus, a little reform can be a very dangerous thing for a repressive regime because it encourages the people to demand further liberalization.

Recent events in the PRC offer further evidence in support of this argument. As discussed in Chapter 3, the economic reforms undertaken by the Beijing government stimulated rapid growth during the 1980s. In less than one decade, the average income of a Chinese citizen doubled. But this rapid growth also brought in its wake economic, social, and political dislocation. Rampant inflation reduced the purchasing power of workers and pensioners with relatively fixed income, thus putting many commodities and social services out of their financial reach. Intellectuals, professionals, and government employees were economic losers in this sense. By comparison, the operators of small private enterprises became prosperous with the new market freedoms. There was therefore an increase in income disparity as well as downward social mobility for some groups and upward social mobility for other groups. At the same time, the dual pricing system for commodities encouraged official corruption, inducing some bureaucrats with special access to state enterprises to purchase commodities at low fixed prices and resell them at higher market prices. These developments produced a widespread sense of frustration and a loss of political confidence in the Communist leadership.

This pent-up frustration produced a massive prodemocracy movement in 1989. For seven weeks, students, workers, and ordinary people marched in the streets of Beijing and other Chinese cities demanding political liberalization and an end to official corruption. These marches coincided with the visit of Mikhail Gorbachev and thus proved to be a serious source of embarrassment for the Chinese leaders. Because many foreign correspondents were in Beijing covering Gorbachev's visit, the demonstrators had an opportunity to present their case to a worldwide audience. The management of this political crisis split the top leaders into two camps, with that of the moderates headed by the secretary-general of the Communist Party, Zhao Ziyang, and that of the hard-liners represented by the aging de facto leader, Deng Xiaoping, and Premier Li Peng. In the ensuing struggle for power, the latter group prevailed.

On June 4, 1989, the People's Liberation Army (PLA) was ordered to clear Tiananmen Square, where the prodemocracy demonstrators had congregated. When the soldiers met resistance, they used firearms to disperse the demonstrators. In the ensuing bloody crackdown, thousands of people were killed. Many leading participants of this movement were imprisoned, and others managed to escape to the United States and France. Although successful in restoring the hard-liners' political control in the short run, this crackdown failed to address the social, economic, and political problems that had originally ignited the popular unrest. Because many top Chinese leaders are already in their eighties, they cannot hope to maintain their political control for very much longer. Therefore, it is likely that similar political instability will recur to challenge the next generation of Chinese leaders.

The PRC has had to pay a heavy price for its bloody crackdown. Previously, foreign investors had been attracted because of the country's ostensible political stability. The events during the spring and summer of 1989 cast serious doubts on this assumption. By the same token, the ruthless suppression of political dissent seriously undermined political confidence at home and abroad. One barometer of this loss of confidence was shown by the Hong Kong stock market, where the value of equities fell by 22 percent on the Monday following the Tiananmen massacre. For three consecutive weekends, one million people—about one-fifth of Hong Kong's population—turned out to demonstrate against the suppression in Beijing. Few Hong Kong residents were inclined to believe Beijing's promises that it would maintain the colony's economic system for fifty years after the PRC took political control of Hong Kong. Instead, there was a stampede to apply for immigrant visas by people who wanted to relocate to the United States, Canada, Australia, and other English-speaking countries. Similarly, Beijing's effort to bring about national reunification with Taiwan undoubtedly suffered a serious setback. Beijing's promise to keep "one country, two systems" (that is, socialism for the Mainland and capitalism for Taiwan within one united China) became less credible.

The 1989 political events in the PRC remind us again that rapid economic growth is likely to erode rather than promote political stability. Moreover, in the wake of economic reforms, there are bound to be rising demands for political reforms. The Chinese leadership has sought to encourage economic liberalization while resisting political liberalization. The carnage on Tiananmen Square has been the most visible, though hardly the only or even the most important, consequence of this contradiction. It is interesting to note that under Mikhail Gorbachev's campaigns of *perestroika* (restructuring) and *glasnost* (openness), political liberalization has preceded economic liberalization. Economic conditions in the USSR have in fact deteriorated during his administration. Therefore, the experiences of these two Communist countries show that economic and political reforms are so closely connected that it is hard to have one without the other. Instead, to borrow a Chinese saying, it is necessary to "walk on two legs."

REGIME INSTABILITY, HUMAN RIGHTS, AND STRATEGIC ALIGNMENT

There was a widespread sense of outrage in the West against the Chinese leaders' crackdown on the prodemocracy demonstrators. The United States, Japan, and other Western countries suspended various political, commercial, and military exchanges with Beijing as a sign of their disapproval. Thus, for example, President George Bush announced that he would temporarily suspend both U.S. arms sales to the PRC and high-level official visits to that country. He also approved the extension of visas for more than 40,000 Chinese citizens (mostly students and exchange scholars) in the United States who might face political persecution if forced to return to their homeland in the near future.

By and large, however, the Western furor was short-lived. Led by the Japanese, foreign businesspeople returned to the PRC after a brief absence. Stories about Beijing's repression of the dissident movement soon disappeared from newspapers or were relegated to back pages. More significant, the official sanctions imposed by the Western governments were quite mild. There was a strong sense in Western official circles that these sanctions should be tempered lest they jeopardize the PRC's recent turn to the West. This sentiment was especially noticeable in Washington and Tokyo, whose leaders wanted to preserve their strategic and commercial ties with Beijing. Thus, for example, just one month after his highly publicized decision to suspend high-level contact with Chinese officials, President Bush had already sent his national security adviser to Beijing on a secret mission.

These Western reactions to the Tiananmen crackdown highlight a recurrent policy dilemma: Should Western governments give priority to the promotion of human rights and political liberalization, or should they place more emphasis on the preservation of friendly, albeit domestically unpopular, regimes? Time and again, Washington faced this choice when mass unrest threatened to overthrow authoritarian but pro-American leaders (e.g., the shah of Iran, Syngman Rhee of South Korea, Ngo Dinh-diem of South Vietnam, Anastasio Somoza of Nicaragua, and, most recently, Ferdinand Marcos of the Philippines). In each case, these leaders had become closely identified with U.S. interests, and vice versa. And in each case, the domestic unpopularity of these leaders became a source of anti-Americanism. Even in those cases where Washington belatedly abandoned its longtime ally in favor of some reformist group, this change of heart often came too late (e.g., in Iran, Nicaragua) to avoid the anti-American backlash.

Although the makers of U.S. foreign policy profess an idealistic commitment to human rights and democracy, all too often they seem to be more concerned about the avoidance of political turmoil and the rise to power of leftist elements in the Third World countries. Washington usually comes down on the side of the "known devil" (i.e., the regime that it has been doing business with) rather than the "unknown devil" (some unfamiliar opposition group). Hence, there is an inherent bureaucratic bias that prefers order to "chaos" and continuity to change— even in face of strong evidence showing that the status quo cannot be sustained or that it is fraught with undesirable consequences. Additionally, although recognizing the faults and foibles of its allies, U.S. leaders often let their cold war mentality cloud their judgments. Thus, in justifying U.S. support for an unpopular South Vietnamese leader in the 1960s, President Lyndon Johnson reportedly remarked that he was after all "our boy" and the "only one we got."

One such close U.S. client was Ferdinand Marcos of the Philippines. Economic stagnation, official corruption, and ineffective government administration made him an increasingly unpopular leader. He managed to hold on to power through martial law, electoral fraud, and political cronyism until the assassination of an opposition leader galvanized and united his opposition. In 1983, when Benigno Aquino was returning home from political exile in the United States and was still in police custody, he was shot on the airport tarmac. This event enraged the Filipino people, who widely suspected Marcos's complicity in this plot to eliminate a popular political rival. They turned out in massive numbers to demand Marcos's resignation. They also rallied behind the candidacy of Corazon Aquino, the widow of the assassinated opposition leader, in the ensuing presidential election. The opposition movement enjoyed the support of the urban middle class, the intellectuals, and the church leaders. When in February 1986 the top military generals announced that they had joined the opposition, Marcos was forced to resign and go into exile in the United States (where he died in 1989). With the departure of Marcos, Corazon Aquino became the president of the Philippines.

All, however, is not well in the Philippines. The country is still gripped by economic stagnation and a wide social gulf between the haves and the have-nots. The conservative elite, called the sugar bloc because of its traditional power base in the ownership of sugarcane plantations, still enjoys considerable influence. Moreover, the anti-Marcos leaders have become badly divided, so that the new government has often been unable to undertake effective policies to deal with the country's pressing socioeconomic problems—on top of two ongoing armed insurgencies, one led by the Communists and the other by Muslim separatists. Finally, the military establishment is splintered, and there have been recurrent plots by the right-wing officers to overthrow the civilian authority. In December 1989, the Aquino government was threatened again by dissident soldiers, who had seized important military installations, communications stations, and tourist hotels in downtown Manila. The rebel forces were persuaded to surrender only after the U.S. Air Force had intervened to prevent antigovernment warplanes from taking off from airfields under rebel control.

In the coming years, the Philippines may be faced with the danger of renewed social unrest and political instability, which would in turn pose a serious policy dilemma for Washington. The United States has been more deeply involved in the affairs of the Philippines, which was once an American colony, than it has in any other Asian country. The Clark Air Base and the Subic Naval Base provide the critical underpinning for the forward deployment of U.S. forces in the Pacific. The bases are in a strategic position to control the vital transit routes connecting Southeast Asia, Oceania, and Northeast Asia. They also enable the monitoring of Soviet ships operating out of their naval bases at Camranh Bay in Vietnam. Therefore, developments in the Philippines may force Washington to make a tough choice between its strategic interests and its democratic ideals; these policy goals may not always coincide as they did in the coup attempt of December 1989.

SOCIAL TRANQUILITY, POLITICAL PLURALISM, AND ECONOMIC STAGNATION

I argued earlier that rapid economic growth may have among its consequences social unrest, political disorder, and repressive regimes. I now reverse the causal sequence and argue that the nature and extent of sociopolitical order can also affect economic growth. It is significant that, according to some perspectives, social peace, political stability, and representative governments based on competitive electoral politics can have a negative rather than a positive influence on economic performance.

What can account for such an outcome? In stable democratic countries, individuals join various groups, and these groups in turn lobby for favorable treatment of their members by the government. The longer a society has enjoyed uninterrupted peace and the freedom of political assembly and organization, the more numerous and entrenched interest groups it should have. Called **distributional coalitions,**[6] these groups try to promote and protect their members' economic and social interests—often at the expense of society at large. Labor unions, professional associations, and producer cartels are just some examples of distributional coalitions. They adopt a variety of practices—such as union "closed shops," cumbersome certification and licensing procedures for professionals (doctors, lawyers, engineers), pricing collusion and market-sharing agreements by manufacturers—that impede the efficient operation of market forces. These practices are intended to fix wages and prices, reduce competition (by making it more difficult for others to join the profession, by banning advertisement for lawyers' or doctors' fees), and contrive scarcity (by limiting supply). This kind of collusion dampens and retards economic innovation and moves the arena of competition from the marketplace to the government office (that is to say, instead of competing for the customers' business by developing a better and cheaper product, the special interests spend their time and energy on lobbying officials for more favorable legislation and regulation).

The accumulation of these interest groups has been described as a case of progressive "institutional sclerosis." The impulses for technological innovation, capital formation, and entrepreneurial initiatives become increasingly suffocated in the straitjacket of self-serving rules and complicated regulations propagated by the labor unions, professional associations, business groups, and, indeed, government bureaucrats. This phenomenon has been described somewhat facetiously as the "British disease" in explanations of the steady decline of that country's industrial competitiveness and global economic position.

Britain, of course, is the classic example of a liberal democracy characterized by pluralistic politics, parliamentary rule, competitive parties, and electoral contests. To varying degrees, the other English-speaking democracies—such as the United States, Canada, Australia, and New Zealand—have followed the main features of the British political system. The political freedoms enjoyed by the citizens of these countries facilitate the organization of interest groups, which have relatively open and easy access to politicians and bureaucrats. In addition, long-term social peace and political order make possible the formation and proliferation of such distributional coalitions over time.

Pluralistic politics, almost by definition, means that there are many groups competing for power and that none of the groups has sufficient power to dominate the political process. The hallmark of pluralistic politics is "win some, lose some" (that is, no one can expect to win all the time). Under this system, policies are made on the basis of compromise, logrolling and pork barrel (you scratch my back, and I'll scratch yours), and shifting voting coalitions (someone who supports you on an issue today may vote against you on a different issue tomorrow). Finally, the imperative of winning elections encourages the political parties to cater to and please as many special interests as possible. Because these parties are relatively evenly balanced in their electoral strength, small shifts in voter sentiments can mean the difference between victory and defeat.

What does all this mean for economic growth? First, in contrast to capitalist East Asia's strong developmental states, the English-speaking pluralistic democracies in the Pacific region—specifically, the United States, Canada, Australia, and New Zealand—have relatively weak regulatory states that are more open and susceptible to the demands from various social groups. Thus, whereas in East Asia the state provides administrative guidance to business and labor, in the English-speaking democracies business and labor lobby the state for favorable policies. Second, the states of pluralistic democracies are fragmented in the sense that the different parts of a government may often be in disagreement over particular issues. This is exemplified, in the case of the United States, by the frequent policy stalemates between a congress dominated by one political party and a presidency headed by the leader of another political party. Third, industrial and monetary policies tend to be made on the basis of short-term political compromises and electoral expediency instead of on the basis of long-term economic sense. And fourth, neither the policymakers nor the policies have much staying power. Politicians come and go as a result of changing electoral fortunes, and policies are negotiated and renegotiated following recurrent rounds of coalition making and coalition breaking.

This lack of continuity in either personnel or policy is a result of **electoral cycling,** the tendency for officials with different political persuasions and policy inclinations to alternate the control of government as a result of changing electoral outcomes.[7] Thus, the two major parties in the United States, Canada, Australia, and New Zealand alternate the control of government, each time instituting a series of policies that can be quite different from those of the preceding administration. In contrast, Japan, Taiwan, and Singapore have all had the same ruling party (the Liberal Democratic Party, the Kuomintang, and the People's Action Party respectively) for three or even four decades. In the case of Hong Kong, the British colonial government and a strong banking cartel provide the same political continuity.

If the above line of reasoning is correct, there is a trade-off between social peace, political stability, and pluralistic democracy on the one hand and economic expansion on the other. The evidence from the Pacific region is at the least not incompatible with this interpretation. The average annual rate of growth in gross national product (GNP) per capita during 1965–1986 was 1.6 percent for the United States, 1.5 percent for New Zealand, 1.7 percent for Australia, and 2.6 percent for Canada.[8] Among the developed industrialized countries, only Switzerland (1.4 percent), Ireland (1.7 percent), and Britain (1.7 percent) had a comparable or even lower growth record. In contrast, Japan's rate of annual economic growth during the same period was 4.3 percent, whereas Hong Kong (6.2 percent), South Korea (6.7 percent), Taiwan (7.0 percent), and Singapore (7.6 percent) turned in even more impressive performances. To varying degrees, the latter countries all exhibit "soft" authoritarianism and, as discussed in Chapter 3, have suppressed organized labor as a political voice. At the same time, the ruling elites of these capitalist East Asian countries have been relatively immune from societal pressure and from electoral cycling.

WAR TRAUMA, INCOME EQUALITY, AND THE PHOENIX FACTOR

Distributional coalitions tend to form under conditions of social stability and political freedom. Conversely, social upheavals, political suppression, and military conflicts tend to undermine and destroy these groups. The United States, Canada, Australia, and New Zealand as well as the slower-growing European countries such as Switzerland and Britain have all enjoyed social tranquility, political order, and constitutional continuity for a long period of time. Moreover, they have also been relatively free from the socioeconomic devastation caused by domestic or foreign war on their territories. They also have not been the victims of political intervention and domination of a foreign occupation authority in the recent past.

In contrast, as discussed in Chapter 2, Japan, Korea, and China (including Taiwan) all suffered from devastating civil and/or foreign war during the 1940s and 1950s. Their economies and societies were deeply traumatized by these experiences, during which many distributional coalitions (the landlords, the industrial unions, the giant business complexes known as *zaibatsu*) were broken up, muzzled, or weakened. At different times and under different circumstances, these countries also came under foreign military occupation (China by Japanese forces; Korea by Japanese, Chinese, and U.S. forces; and Japan by U.S. forces). This foreign military occupation often weakened the power of traditional elites opposed to economic or political reforms, thereby serving as a catalyst for these countries' subsequent industrialization effort.

Traumatic internal or external war sometimes also helps to pressure incumbent elites to undertake important socioeconomic reforms. Thus, for example, the Taiwanese and South Korean governments, overwhelmingly defeated at the hands of the Communists and pressured by U.S. advisers, were finally moved to initiate land reforms in their territorial remnants. These land reforms, as discussed earlier, led to the rise in agricultural productivity that in turn provided the capital surplus for industrialization. At the same time, the reforms provided the foundation for an egalitarian society in which the income disparity between the rich and the poor is kept relatively low.

The above argument suggests that, paradoxically, civil war and foreign occupation may contribute to a loosening of the grip of distributional coalitions on economic production and social allocation. That is, the social upheavals and political disorders resulting from these traumas may have a therapeutic effect in "unblocking" previously "blocked" production resources and in dismantling social institutions that undermine productivity as well as equity. A number of researchers have in fact found a pattern indicating that the defeated countries in a major foreign war tend to have faster economic growth subsequently than the victorious countries. This pattern has been called the **phoenix factor** (alluding to the rise of this legendary bird from its own ashes). It provides at least a partial explanation for the rapid recovery and then ascendance of the German and Japanese economies after World War II and the relative stagnation of the British, French, and U.S. economies.

In the Pacific region, Australia, New Zealand, Canada, and the United States have indeed had lower economic growth rates than their capitalist East Asian counterparts. The former countries also happened to be the military victors in World War II; they have also enjoyed long-term social peace and political stability, which provide a conducive climate for the formation and proliferation of distributional coalitions. In contrast, Japan, South Korea, Taiwan, Hong Kong, and Singapore have all suffered from military conflict, foreign occupation, and/or colonial rule. These countries, moreover, have had much higher rates of economic growth. Thus, the developmental histories of these two sets of countries since the 1950s seem to conform to the expectation that social peace, political stability, and security from foreign rule may in the long run be accompanied by relative economic stagnation. This evidence, however, does not constitute sufficient proof of the validity of the latter expectation.

Although the relevant evidence is more limited and tentative, the developmental history of the Pacific region seems to support the view that those countries with recent traumas of foreign invasion or civil war tend to have more egalitarian systems of income distribution than countries that did not suffer such traumas.[9] It may surprise some readers that the capitalist East Asian countries, despite their suppression of organized labor and their low government support for social welfare, have actually achieved greater income equality than the advanced Western countries. For example, as shown in Table 4.1, the richest 20 percent of the Taiwanese population claimed 37.3 percent of that country's national wealth (in 1982), whereas 8.7 percent of the national wealth went to the poorest 20 percent of the population. In South Korea the

Table 4.1
Cross-National Patterns of Income Distribution: Percent of National Income Accrued by Each Population Quintile

		Bottom 20%	Second 20%	Third 20%	Fourth 20%	Top 20%
Low-income countries						
Bangladesh	1981-1982	6.6	10.7	15.3	22.1	45.3
India	1975-1976	7.0	9.2	13.9	20.5	49.4
Kenya	1976	2.6	6.3	11.5	19.2	60.4
Sri Lanka	1980-1981	5.8	10.1	14.1	20.3	49.8
Zambia	1976	3.4	7.4	11.2	16.9	61.1
Lower-middle-income countries						
Egypt	1974	5.8	10.7	14.7	20.8	48.0
Indonesia	1976	6.6	7.8	12.6	23.6	49.4
Ivory Coast	1985-1986	2.4	6.2	10.9	19.1	61.4
Peru	1972	1.9	5.1	11.0	21.0	61.0
Philippines	1985	5.2	8.9	13.2	20.2	52.5
Thailand	1975-1976	5.6	9.6	13.9	21.1	49.8
Turkey	1973	3.5	8.0	12.5	19.5	56.5
Upper-middle-income countries						
Argentina	1970	4.4	9.7	14.1	21.5	50.3
Brazil	1972	2.0	5.0	9.4	17.0	66.6
Malaysia	1973	3.5	7.7	12.4	20.3	56.1
Hong Kong	1980	5.4	10.8	15.2	21.6	47.0
Israel	1979-1980	6.0	12.0	17.7	24.4	39.9
Mexico	1977	2.9	7.0	12.0	20.4	57.7
South Korea	1976	5.7	11.2	15.4	22.4	45.3
Taiwan	1982	8.7	13.8	17.6	22.7	37.3
Venezuela	1970	3.0	7.3	12.9	22.8	54.0
Industrial market economies						
Australia	1975-1976	5.4	10.0	15.0	22.5	47.1
Canada	1981	5.3	11.8	18.0	24.9	40.0
France	1975	5.5	11.5	17.1	23.7	42.2
West Germany	1978	7.9	12.5	17.0	23.1	39.5
Japan	1979	8.7	13.2	17.5	23.1	37.5
New Zealand	1981-1982	5.1	10.8	16.2	23.2	44.7
Sweden	1981	7.4	13.1	16.8	21.0	41.7
United Kingdom	1979	7.0	11.5	17.0	24.8	39.7
United States	1980	5.3	11.9	17.9	25.0	39.9

Sources: World Bank, *World Development Report 1988* (New York: Oxford University Press, 1988), pp. 272–273; and Council for Economic Planning and Development, *Taiwan Statistical Data Book* (Taipei: author, 1987), p. 62.

income shares of the richest and poorest quintiles of the population were 5.7 percent and 45.3 percent respectively (in 1976), whereas the comparable figures for Hong Kong (in 1980) were 5.4 percent and 47.0 percent.[10] In Japan the poorest 20 percent of the people received 8.7 percent of all income (in 1979), whereas the wealthiest 20 percent received 37.5 percent.

In comparison, the wealthier people in the United States, Canada, Australia, and New Zealand have been getting a much larger slice of the national income, and the poorer people in these countries have been receiving a smaller share. The income shares of the richest 20 percent of the people were 39.9 percent for the United States (in 1980), 40.0 percent for Canada (in 1981), 47.1 percent for Australia (in 1975–1976), and 44.7 percent for New Zealand (in 1981–1982). Thus, the rich in these countries tend to be much more privileged than the rich in the capitalist East Asian countries, except for South Korea. The income shares of the poorest fifth of the population in the English-speaking Pacific Rim democracies were 5.3 percent for the United States, 5.3 percent for Canada, 5.4 percent for Australia, and 5.1 percent for New Zealand. Consequently, the poor in these democracies have been comparatively (as opposed to being absolutely) worse off than their counterparts in capitalist East Asia.

If one recalls that with the exception of Japan, the East Asian countries have had much lower levels of average income and have not had any elected national governments comparable to those of the English-speaking democracies, this empirical pattern regarding income distribution is rather striking. Put succinctly, contrary to what one might have expected, the liberal democracies have not led to a more equal system of income distribution. In fact, the more authoritarian and less representative East Asian governments have been able to produce higher levels of income equality as well as economic growth. This is a rather impressive feat when we consider two factors. First, as we have seen, cross-national and historical research has shown that rapid economic growth tends at least initially to undermine income equality.[11] Second, because the capitalist East Asian regimes have engaged in a variety of practices that suppress organized labor and keep wages and social welfare low, their egalitarian income systems would again be rather unexpected.

To conclude, one cannot assume that social peace, political stability, and liberal democratic institutions necessarily produce faster economic growth or more egalitarian income distribution. On the contrary, the evidence from the Pacific region suggests that peace, stability, and pluralistic politics may carry a hidden price tag. Countries characterized by these features tend to have stronger and more numerous distributional coalitions and are more susceptible to policy stalemate and electoral cycling. Conversely, war, revolution, and foreign occupation seem to have had a therapeutic effect on the capitalist East Asian countries by stimulating reforms that in turn have produced an unusual combination of growth with equity.

DEFENSE BURDEN
AND ECONOMIC PERFORMANCE

We have just seen that disastrous policy performance in the management of external security (leading to war, military defeat, and even foreign occupation) sometimes can prompt important domestic changes that lead subsequently to economic expansion and social equity. However, high defense expenditures in the quest for military security are more likely than not to impair economic performance.

A heavy defense burden can affect economic performance as a result of three main processes. First, military spending tends to hurt the savings and investment rates, which in turn are major determinants of future economic growth. A government can finance its military spending through taxation, borrowing, or printing more money. High taxation takes from the citizens wealth that would otherwise be consumed, saved, or invested and puts it in the government's hands. Government borrowing (e.g., through U.S. treasury bills) leaves less capital available for business investment, and in order to compete with the government for the available capital, the business community has to pay a higher interest rate. Finally, if a government increases the money supply faster than productivity grows, inflationary pressure will mount in the long run. The fear of future inflation will encourage people to spend and borrow instead of to save (if the inflation rate and taxation rate are higher than the interest rate for savings, the money saved will actually buy less in the future). Thus, defense expenditures can make capital scarcer and more expensive, depriving industries of the funds necessary for future expansion and innovation.

Second, defense spending in the advanced industrial countries is often capital and technology intensive. Such spending diverts resources from the civilian sector, thus handicapping the latter's international competitiveness. According to some estimates, about half the engineers and scientists in the United States have been employed by the defense and space industries. There has therefore been a relative shortage of human resources devoted to research and development of new civilian products. Given the increasing interdependence and competition among different national economies, often a country's most dynamic and leading industries are in the export sector—such as for automobiles, machines, electronics, and information-processing and communications systems. These export-oriented civilian industries frequently serve as the engine of growth that pulls the rest of the economy along. They fall into those market niches where international competition is fierce and technological innovation is constantly taking place. They also happen, however, to produce the equipment that a modern military would be most interested in. Therefore, defense procurement is most likely to crowd out or dampen civilian work in these industries. This procurement tends to create production bottlenecks, material shortages, and especially limited human resources for the innovation of civilian technologies.

The line of reasoning just presented argues that miliary spending (especially if it is capital and technology intensive) takes resources away from the most dynamic civilian industries. Over time this deprivation of resources produces a decline in the vitality and competitiveness of the export sector, which in turn means slower economic growth. Rising imports and falling exports produce trade deficits. If not properly managed, this situation eventually leads to domestic unemployment and currency devaluation (employment suffers as a result of sagging overseas demand for one's exports, while the value of one's currency declines as foreigners become reluctant to hold ever-increasing amounts of this currency as payment for their exports). This situation can also result in a large share of the domestic market and production runs being captured by foreign manufacturers (see the example of the automobile industry in Chapter 3).

Third, and in contrast to the preceding two processes, it has been argued by some analysts that a heavy defense burden can have some positive effects on the economy. The capital investments by the military can improve a country's infrastructure in transportation and communication (airports, railways); government purchases of defense items can stimulate production and encourage fuller utilization of existing facilities; and military training equips recruits with modern skills and attitudes and can, therefore, improve a developing society's human resources for industrialization. These positive effects of a heavy defense burden are seen to offset the negative effects mentioned earlier.

On balance, the evidence is more supportive of the first two processes than of the third one.[12] For the developed countries especially, there is a rather strong pattern suggesting a negative relationship between the degree of defense burden and the rate of economic growth. That is, countries that spend a higher percentage of their GNP on defense have had lower rates of economic expansion. Conversely, countries with a lighter defense burden have tended to grow faster economically. The evidence seems quite strong in indicating that military expenditures tend to dampen capital formation and undercut export competitiveness. Furthermore, unless there is a surplus production capacity (which is usually not the case in developing countries), these expenditures are more likely to result in production bottlenecks than fuller capacity utilization. Finally, whether in the case of infrastructural investment or personnel training, it is almost always cheaper and more efficient to fund civilian projects directly with these purposes in mind than to hope that the desired effects will come indirectly through military spending. Thus, the net effect of the defense burden on economic growth seems to be generally negative.

In regard to the Pacific region, much has been said about the different experiences of Japan and the United States. The former country has been spending about 1 percent of its GNP on defense, whereas the latter country has been committing about 6.5 percent to that purpose during recent years. Concomitantly (and as seen before), the Japanese economy has been growing at a rate that is more than 2.5 times faster than that of the U.S. economy. Consequently, there is a sense that Japan's relatively light defense burden has helped its economic expansion, whereas the relatively heavy defense burden of the United States has hampered its economic performance. Since officials in Washington feel that U.S. military spending has enhanced the security of U.S. allies, they see Japan as a free rider that has not contributed its fair share of the costs of collective defense.

A light defense burden, however, provides only a partial explanation of the superior economic performances of the capitalist East Asian countries. Relatively heavy defense burdens have been borne by Singapore (just above 5 percent of its GNP in the mid-1980s), Taiwan (between 8.0 and 4.6 percent), and South Korea (between 5.8 and 4.8 percent). Indeed, during the 1950s and 1960s Taiwan and South Korea devoted a much higher proportion (over 10 percent) of their GNP to defense, thus putting them among the top military spenders (relative to the size of their economy) in the world. Nevertheless, these East Asian NICs do not appear to have been severely handicapped by their heavy defense burdens in the drive for economic development. As discussed before, they have sustained rapid economic growth at a pace that few in the developed or the developing world can match.

Why did this happen? This achievement was facilitated in part by massive U.S. economic aid, which offset or ameliorated the negative effects of Taiwan's and South Korea's heavy defense burden on their respective economies. The United States also provided large amounts of military aid to these countries during the 1950s and 1960s. In the absence of this aid, the defense burden of the East Asians would have been even heavier. To a lesser extent, British military spending in the Far East had the same effect for Singapore.

In Chapter 3, we discussed the suppression of industrial wages and the low levels of spending for social overhead in the capitalist East Asian countries. To a significant extent, these countries tried to fund the military establishment by trimming government subsidies for social welfare. In contrast, the pluralistic competitive politics of the United

States has usually prompted politicians and officials to promise both "guns and butter." Thus, with the exception of the years of Ronald Reagan's presidency, federal expenditures for military as well as civilian programs have risen simultaneously.[13] This reluctance to "bite the bullet" of fiscal trade-offs and/or to raise taxes has led to increasingly large budget deficits. In the case of the Reagan administration, however, the increases in military spending were so huge and the government's revenues so inadequate that the federal deficit became larger than ever before. It is clear that a government's policies toward the procurement of "guns," "butter," and taxes can have profound effects on macroeconomic performances with respect to inflation, unemployment, capital investment, human resources, and export competitiveness.

POLITICAL SUBORDINATION, COMMERCIAL EXCHANGES, AND SECURITY BLANKET

The capitalist East Asian countries are dependent on a steady and reliable supply of reasonably priced raw materials from overseas sources and need easy and uninterrupted access to consumer markets abroad. Additionally, they search for investment opportunities in foreign countries to secure resource supply and market access. Even though they have relatively large military establishments and defense hardware that is rather sophisticated by Third World standards (or, in the case of Japan, by the standards of the industrialized countries), these countries are hardly in a current position to "go it alone." Military autonomy has not been in the past and is not likely to be in the future a realistic or desirable policy option for them.

There are several potential sources of military threat to the capitalist East Asian countries. The North Korean government in Pyongyang is one such possible though unlikely source. If another armed conflict between the rival regimes on the Korean peninsula were to take place, it could involve all the four major powers (the United States, the USSR, the PRC, and Japan). The geographic proximity of the Korean peninsula to the Chinese and Japanese homelands and their respective urban and industrial centers means that any war in Korea would be a matter of grave concern for Beijing and Tokyo. However, the danger of such a war seems to have abated in the recent years. Both Beijing and Moscow have sent clear signals to Pyongyang indicating that they would not welcome renewed military tension between Pyongyang and Seoul, thus restraining their North Korean ally. Moreover, the balance of power favors South Korea and should discourage a frontal military attack by North Korea. South Korea's population is twice as large as North Korea's, and its economy is four times larger.

Another continuing source of possible military tension is Indochina, where Vietnam aspires to become a subregional power. It has substantial influence over the ruling regimes in Laos and Cambodia. Indeed, the current government in Phnom Penh was installed with the help of a Vietnamese invasion force (which overthrew the notorious Khmer Rouge regime of Pol Pot). The civil war between this regime and a coalition of opposition forces has gone on since the late 1970s. In this civil war, the Vietnamese have supported the current Cambodian regime, whereas the Chinese, Thais, and Americans have offered various forms of aid to the armed resistance groups. The 1989 decision by Hanoi to pull its troops out of Cambodia has eased tension somewhat in this area.

Although the PRC has a large standing army, it has a very limited capability to undertake large-scale military operation beyond its borders. In 1979, Beijing carried out a short-lived campaign against Vietnam in retaliation for the latter's invasion of Cambodia, then under the control of the Chinese-backed Pol Pot regime. This campaign exposed the weaknesses of the Chinese armed forces: They lacked modern communications, logistics, and armament. The budget and personnel of the PLA were further trimmed during the 1980s, when economic modernization received Beijing's top priority. Thus, the PLA, despite its large size, is still primarily a defensive force that is ill equipped for sustained foreign operation away from its home base.

This leaves the USSR as the most potent military threat faced by the capitalist East Asians. Operating from bases in eastern Siberia and Vietnam, Soviet planes and ships can threaten vital sea-lanes connecting Japan, South Korea, Taiwan, and Singapore to their trade partners. Because none of these countries possesses the means of coping with this threat, they seek security from U.S. military protection. U.S. forces stationed in the Pacific and the U.S. nuclear arsenal provide the necessary deterrent to Soviet aggression.

In order to counterbalance the Soviet threat as well as to reduce their dependence on the United States, Japan, Thailand, the Philippines, and even South Korea have recently sought to establish friendlier relations with Beijing. The Japanese, in particular, have made a major effort to consolidate their ties with the PRC through commercial trade, developmental assistance, capital investment, and technology transfer. Similarly, Manila and especially Bangkok have engaged in political exchanges and military consultation with Beijing. And despite their ostensible ideological differences, trade between the PRC and South Korea has been growing steadily. Thus, all these countries have tried to play the "China card" as a way of promoting both their military security and commercial expansion.

In recent years, South Korea's and especially Japan's attention has also been attracted to the vast resources of Soviet Siberia. The petroleum, natural gas, copper, and timber in this region offer a nearby source of supply for the resource-hungry industries of these two East Asian countries, a source that would let them reduce their dependence on the more distant supplies in the Middle East and North America. At the same time, Japan could offer the necessary capital and technology—which Moscow does not currently have—to develop this region. This may appear as a mutually attractive business proposition, but it raises some complicating political and military considerations.

A heavy dependence on Soviet raw materials may give Moscow the leverage to demand political concessions. For this reason, Tokyo has tried to limit its imports from the USSR to only about 10 percent of its national needs. At the same time, a Japanese decision to undertake huge multiyear investments in Soviet Siberia will surely raise eyebrows in Beijing and Washington, especially since some projects (e.g., the development of oil resources, the expansion of port facilities, the construction of a transportation system) could have dual civilian and military uses. Japanese involvement in these projects could thus jeopardize Tokyo's political relations with Beijing and Washington. It was reported that Tokyo pulled back from the Tyumen project, the construction of a railroad-pipeline system in Soviet Siberia for transshipping petroleum, because of Beijing's objections to the project's strategic implications.[14] Moreover, in order to soothe Chinese as well as U.S. concerns, the Japanese have made U.S. participation a condition for their involvement in any major joint venture with the USSR to explore and develop Siberia's natural resources (in objecting to the Tyumen project, Chinese officials hinted that they might have tolerated it had the Americans been part of this joint venture).

Thus, contrary to the popular image of the Japanese as purely "economic animals," they have clearly put politics in command in dealing with the USSR. Moscow's refusal to discuss the status of several northern islands that it seized from Japan at the end of World War II continues to be an obstacle to further improvements in their bilateral relations. Additionally, Tokyo's pursuit of comprehensive security—with its heavy emphasis on commercial diplomacy and economic statecraft—would not have been possible without the underpinning of the U.S. military deterrence. The protection of Washington's security blanket permits Tokyo this luxury of pursuing an omnidirectional foreign policy, with a focus on securing export markets, overseas investments, and supplies of raw materials. Similarly, the other capitalist East Asian countries have been to varying degrees incorporated into a U.S.-led security system. Thus far, the implicit bargain has been that they would defer and submit themselves to the political leadership of the United States in its competition with the USSR in return for Washington's military protection and access to the U.S. market.

PUBLIC GOODS, FREE RIDERS, AND THE BURDEN OF HEGEMONY

Economists use the term **public goods** to describe benefits that can be shared noncompetitively. These benefits have two characteristics. First, they are *nondivisible* in the sense that their consumption by one individual does not reduce their consumption by another person. Second, they are *nonexcludable* in the sense that once these goods are provided to any one person, it is impossible or very costly to prevent others from enjoying them. International peace, stability, and order are widely regarded as public goods with those features.

At the same time, the nature of public goods encourages free-riding. If, for example, the North Atlantic Treaty Organization (NATO) provides the public good of deterring Soviet aggression, why should its smaller members (e.g., the Belgians, the Norwegians, the Dutch) provide for their own defense? It would be very difficult to exclude these smaller members—and, indeed, nonmembers such as Switzerland and Sweden—from being the beneficiaries of the resulting peace and stability in Europe (Washington could not very well tell Moscow that it is free to attack the latter countries, thereby undermining its own deterrence effort against possible Soviet aggression). Instead, the smaller members of the alliance would like to rely on the defense forces of the larger members to contain the Soviet threat.[15]

Yet, paradoxically, if every country had withheld its defense contribution in the belief that it could not possibly be excluded from the benefits of a Western alliance, no alliance would have been formed in the first place. Why, then, do collective arrangements for the provision of public goods come about? Some recent explanations dwell on the role of a great power, which has both the incentive and the means to initiate and sustain such arrangements. Only such a great power—called a *hegemon* in the literature—is likely to be willing and able to assume the leadership responsibility and to bear a disproportionate burden in ensuring that public goods are provided. In the absence of such a hegemon, the selfish inclinations of the smaller countries would prevail—and no collective arrangements to supply public goods would be instituted.

A hegemon is supposed to be sufficiently wealthy and powerful to afford a disproportionate amount of the costs for supplying the public good. It is also supposed to have the motivation to provide the public good because, as the wealthiest and most powerful state, it has the greatest vested interest in preserving the existing international order. Therefore, even though the hegemon has to pay more than the others, its benefits from the public good would still be greater than its costs. That is, even though *proportionately* the burden of providing the public good falls heaviest on the hegemon (in the most extreme case, the hegemon may assume the entire costs of the public good), it still is *absolutely* better off with the provision than without the provision of this public good.

More specifically, in the post–World War II era, the United States has been the dominant power that has had both the heaviest stake in and the greatest means for preserving a capitalist world system. Accordingly, the United States, in an attempt to contain communism, was instrumental in developing a network of military alliances along the Soviet and Chinese borders. It was also the leading member and host government for the premier intergovernmental organization, the United Nations. Moreover, the United States exercised a decisive voice in the formation and evolution of various international monetary and trade agreements. The Bretton Woods multilateral accord (1947) provided for a system of fixed exchange rates (within 1 percent of their value pegged to gold). To provide international monetary stability and liquidity, the U.S. government committed itself to convert dollars into gold (at $35 an ounce), thereby making the U.S. dollar the international currency of choice (the convertibility of dollar into gold was withdrawn by President Richard Nixon in 1971).

The United States also took a leading role in formulating the new international commercial order after World War II. The result was the 1947 General Agreement on Tariffs and Trade (GATT). This agreement codified the prevailing consensus on free trade and banned discriminatory commercial practices as well as unilateral trade quotas (note that the VERs discussed in Chapter 3 were supposed to be "voluntary" and thus technically in conformity with the GATT guidelines). GATT laid the foundation for the progressive liberalization of international trade (such as by encouraging the reduction of tariffs and the extension of trade advantages equally to all members of GATT through the "most-favored-nation" clause) in the subsequent two and a half decades. Together these institutions provided public goods in the form of ensuring international peace, deterring military aggression, promoting monetary stability, and encouraging free trade.

During the 1950s and 1960s, the United States contributed disproportionately to the payment of these public goods. For example, as we have seen, it spent a higher percentage of its GNP for defense purposes than its allies did. Similarly, it offered asymmetric market access to the goods of its trade partners and ready convertibility of the dollar (until the early 1970s). In comparison with its allies, the United States bore a much heavier burden in ensuring international peace, Western security, trade liberalization, and monetary stability. The other Western countries were in effect permitted to free-ride (to pay less than their proportionate share of the costs of these public goods). The economic prosperity and military security of the U.S. allies—including West Germany and Japan— would have been rather difficult to imagine in the absence of the international order and stability provided by the U.S. hegemony in the postwar era.

HEGEMONIC DECLINE, POWER TRANSITION, AND INTERNATIONAL ORDER

Over time, a hegemon is apt to suffer a decline in its power.[16] This decline is in part due to the free-riding behavior of the countries that take advantage of the hegemon's generosity, making the hegemon gradually less willing and/or able to continue the asymmetric trade, monetary, or security relationships. The decline is also in part due to the very success of the international political and economic order fostered by the hegemon: Stability and prosperity in the foreign economies encourage businesspeople in the hegemonic country to invest abroad, thereby providing capital to the follower countries and draining capital from the hegemon. The tendency for the elite of the hegemonic country to hold on to outdated beliefs and practices when they are no longer warranted by the new situation further accelerates the power decline.

What happens when the power of the hegemon declines? It becomes less able and/or willing to underwrite the costs of maintaining the international political and economic order that it had earlier instituted. What should happen then? According to the **hegemonic stability theory**— which argues that only the leading global power has the means and the will to provide international order and stability—in the aftermath of a hegemon's slip from dominance, the international system becomes more chaotic and discordant. In the absence of a dominant power to provide public goods, to ensure orderly transactions, and to enforce the rules of international conduct, each country pursues its short-term myopic self-interest. Each undertakes "beggar thy neighbor" policies of trade protectionism, competitive currency devaluation, and economic warfare. Thus, mercantilism replaces commercial liberalism. To some observers, the late 1920s and the early 1930s were characterized by this kind of economic nationalism—which in turn exacerbated the severity of the Great Depression and hastened the onset of World War II.

Politically and militarily, the international system evolves into a classic form of balance of power. Yet in contrast to the hegemonic stability theory, some analysts and officials view this evolution as contributing to international peace. According to the **balance-of-power theory,** international peace is more likely to be maintained when there is a rough balance of capabilities between two or more rival countries or alliances, whereas international war is more likely to occur when one country or alliance has a preponderance of capabilities. In the ideal world described by this theory, each country develops its own military forces instead of relying on the hegemon for its security. It joins and withdraws from various alliance coalitions in order to check the power of any major country that threatens to become the new hegemon. The international system therefore becomes more fluid and less concentrated in its power configuration. It moves from the unipolarity (having one center of power) of a hegemonic order to the multipolarity of several roughly equal contending powers. The latter situation characterized European diplomacy in the years leading to World War I. However, contrary to the expectations of the balance-of-power theory, the trend toward less power concentration and more power parity among the rival countries has tended to increase the magnitude of wars in the twentieth century.[17]

The relationship between the danger of war outbreak and the international distribution of power is a central concern of the **power transition theory.**[18] This theory is more congenial to the proponents of hegemonic stability. According to the power transition theory, the most likely period for major wars to break out is when one great power is overtaking another great power. It is sometimes described as the rear-end collision version of international conflict. Presenting a dynamic view of the genesis of international conflict, this theory stresses the different rates of economic growth and power accumulation on the part of rival countries. International conflict is most likely to occur when the rate of development of the previously leading country is slowing down and when the rate of development of the previously lagging country is accelerating. Under this circumstance, the distance (or gap) between the two countries becomes smaller and the danger of the latecomer bumping into the leader accordingly increases.

In contrast to the balance-of-power theory, the power transition theory argues that wars are unlikely to happen when there is a large disparity between the power of a leading country and that of a challenging country. In this situation, the leading country (the hegemon) can afford to be magnanimous. It also wants to preserve rather than to upset the existing international order with itself as the top dog. In any case, the challenging country does not have the means to alter this order, even though it may be unhappy with it. The challenger would be very hesitant to start a war against a vastly superior enemy because the odds are heavily against the less powerful country's winning this military contest.

Conversely, when the capabilities of the leader and challenger become more evenly balanced, both are more disposed to fight a war. For the leader, its supremacy is at stake (thus, it can no longer afford to be magnanimous or inactive). Moreover, given its own falling rate of growth and the rising rate of growth of the challenger, the leader may decide to precipitate a fight before the balance of power becomes even less favorable to it. At the same time, the challenger, having reduced the gap between itself and the leader, is apt to become cocky and overconfident (once the odds are not so unfavorable to its winning a war). This combination increases the danger of war.

The power transition theory points to the historical timing of World War I and World War II. World War I did not take place when Britain enjoyed a preponderant power edge over its European neighbors. Rather, it happened only after Germany had caught up with Britain. Similarly, World War II took place after the Axis powers (especially Germany and Japan) had reduced the power gap between themselves and the Allied powers (especially Britain and France). By implication, the power transition theory suggests that the hegemonic decline of the United States, along with the rise of Soviet military power and the resurgence of Japanese economic power, may be the harbinger of a less peaceful period in the future.

The hegemonic stability theory and the power transition theory agree that order and stability have tended to accompany those historical periods characterized by the predominance of one great power. In their view, the years of British supremacy (the 1860s and 1870s) and of U.S supremacy (the 1950s and 1960s) were relatively peaceful. Although there were wars during those periods, they were limited in scope and severity and did not transform the international order, as World War I and World War II did. At the same time, "Pax Britannica" and "Pax Americana" provided a political and security climate conducive to the growth of international trade. These were the periods of general trade liberalization.

Conversely, the periods of hegemonic decline or rivalry among several contending powers seem to have been marked by greater political, economic, and military turmoil. During the 1920s and 1930s, when the British were no longer able and the Americans were not yet willing to assume the leadership responsibilities of a hegemon, the international economic order broke down. Each country undertook competitive currency devaluation and imposed exorbitant import tariffs. The "beggar thy neighbor" attitudes of the Western countries intensified international rivalry and discord. Moreover, their mercantilist monetary and trade policies led to economic hardship, political disorder, and financial instability (as exemplified by the hyperinflation in the German Weimar Republic, the public's loss of confidence in its government, the rise of Adolf Hitler, and Germany's aggressions that led to World War II).

PUBLIC GOODS OR PRIVATE GAINS?

U.S. officials and scholars are especially attracted to the hegemonic stability theory. They are apt to associate the perception of a United States less dominant in international affairs with the perception of a world marked by rising political disorder and economic instability. By casting their country in the role of the main or even the sole provider of public goods such as international peace, monetary order, and free trade, Americans give themselves a big share of the credit for the security and prosperity of their allies. In doing so, they also implicitly or explicitly make these allies—especially Japan and West Germany—appear as ungrateful and selfish free riders.

The theories of public goods and hegemonic stability do help to clarify and explain some historical events and developments, such as those cited as evidence in support of these theories in the preceding discussion. However, history is considerably more complex than the arguments and illustrations that I presented earlier. For example, Britain, even at its height, never had the world's biggest GNP or military expenditures.[19] Moreover, Britain did not always press its trade partners for more open trade, nor was it always willing to make tariff concessions to liberalize commerce. The hegemonic stability theory would point to British or U.S. supremacy as the cause of trade liberalization during the late nineteenth century and the mid-twentieth century, with trade liberalization in turn a cause of global economic prosperity. It seems, however, equally plausible to argue from the historical evidence that it was general world prosperity— and not British or U.S. hegemony—that led to trade liberalization, thus reversing the customary causal order presented by the hegemonic stability theory.

An argument could also be made that the ostensible periods of Pax Britannica and Pax Americana were hardly peaceful or stable. Thus, the Crimean War (1854), the Austro-Prussian War (1866), and the Franco-Prussian War (1870) all took place during the days of British dominance, and all of these conflicts involved the major powers of that time. Similarly, even at the height of U.S. hegemony, Washington was unable to prevent— or to win—wars in Korea and Vietnam. Thus, although the superpowers did not find themselves in a direct armed conflict (the closest they came to that was during the Cuban Missile Crisis in 1962) and although there has been general peace among the developed capitalist countries, the period of U.S. world dominance was not entirely peaceful. There were many wars during this period—some of them, such as the Korean and Vietnamese conflicts, were quite protracted and costly in human lives.

This observation in turn naturally raises the question: To what extent have the benefits of hegemonic rule really been public goods? To a significant extent, the benefits of international peace, stability, and prosperity are excludable—and therefore are not pure public goods. These benefits, as suggested above, tend to go to the developed, capitalist, Western countries or to those developing countries that are somehow deemed strategically or symbolically important in Washington's containment policy against international communism. Accordingly, much of Asia, Africa, and Latin America was excluded from the benefits of peace, stability, and prosperity. Those areas were left out of the strategic alliances, the foreign assistance programs, and the international trade and monetary arrangements made among the developed Western countries or between them and their strategic clients in the Third World. Indeed, some Third World advocates—especially those who hold the dependency perspective (see Chapter 3)—would argue that the prosperity of the developed countries has been precisely due to their exploitation of and dominance over the developing countries. In this sense, then, economic prosperity and development are divisible—that is to say, they are not public goods because they do not fulfill the requirement of nondivisibility. According to this view, the prosperity and well-being of those few members of the exclusive Western club have been based on the denial of these same benefits to the very many nonclub countries.

Thus, hegemonic rule does not necessarily produce public goods for all countries. Indeed, it can produce considerable private goods for the hegemon. In the words of one noted scholar, "If one looks not at narrow issue-area regimes but at broader aspects of the international environment after World War II, one has to be impressed by the degree to which perceived American interests, not just the interests of all states, were served."[20]

With few exceptions (e.g., Cuba, South Vietnam), the *cordon sanitaire* (quarantine line) imposed by the U.S.-led military and political alliance around the USSR and the PRC did succeed in containing communism. The decolonization of previous European and Japanese possessions in the Third World did open their markets to U.S. goods and investment and provide U.S. access to their raw materials. The United States, as the world's most productive economy, largest foreign investor, and leading technological power, benefited far more than its commercial rivals from the freer trade during the 1950s and 1960s. Naturally, the preservation of peace and the containment of communism helped to sustain U.S. access to the foreign markets and sources of raw materials. And even though the United States paid more dollars than its allies for military deterrence against Communist expansion, its allies often paid more in real estate and human lives. Last but not least, the United States was able to achieve a global dominance in cultural influence with the spread of the English language, U.S.-style education, and the "American way of life" (called sometimes "coca-colonization"). These considerations led a well-known international relations scholar to conclude that "the characterization of hegemonic America as predominantly supplying itself and others with collective [i.e., public] goods is inaccurate. Even for those goods which can correctly be called collective the United States has not paid at all disproportionate costs."[21] Indeed, these costs have been "recouped many times over" by offsetting gains.

One of the most memorable quotes attributed to Louis XV of France was *"après moi, le déluge"* (after me, chaos). There is a certain feeling that Americans are inclined to treat the perceived decline of their country in international economics and politics in a similar manner. Yet, has there indeed been a loss of U.S. influence in world affairs, and if so, how great and how precipitous has been this decline? If there has been a relative or absolute decline in U.S. power, what are the main causes for it: the free-riding behavior of its ungrateful allies or the imprudent policies of Washington's own officials? Finally, should we expect chaos, disorder, and instability to follow necessarily in the wake of a less dominant United States? We shall turn to these and other questions regarding the future of the Pacific region in Chapter 5.

CONCLUSION

In this chapter I have argued that the goals of economic growth, sociopolitical order, and military and resource security are not related in simple, linear, and mutually reinforcing ways. The hope that these values would somehow form a virtuous cycle, upon closer inspection, turns out to be just that—a hope rather than an accurate reflection of a complex reality.

Milton Friedman, a Nobel laureate in economics, has been quoted as saying that there is no free lunch in this world. For every policy goal there are obvious as well as hidden costs. Oftentimes, the pursuit of the goals of growth, order, and security has unintended and undesirable side effects, thereby creating a deleterious feedback circuit. Thus, for instance, rapid economic growth can undermine the existing sociopolitical order, whereas a stable sociopolitical system can paradoxically hinder the potential for rapid economic growth. Similarly, the pursuit of security through heavy military spending can impair economic growth. Nevertheless, as we shall discuss in Chapter 5, economic growth can in turn increase the pressure on policymakers to seek foreign economic or military expansion, thus increasing international tension and the danger of war. The presence of such tension or trade-offs among alternative goals constantly challenges officials. It is a perennial source of policy dilemma that demands careful choice and continuous adjustment.

FIVE

□　□　□

Looking Forward:
Alternative Futures

T he preceding chapters explored some salient features of the political
and economic history of selected Pacific Rim countries. I tried to
compare and contrast the main differences in their historical experiences
and to present alternative explanations for these differences. Let us now
turn our attention to discerning what the future holds for the Pacific
region. The evidence and implications for change as well as stasis will
be considered. I shall outline several models of the future in order to
help us to sharpen our thinking about alternative developments (some
of which are more likely than others) in this region.

PERSISTENT DOMINANCE
OR LOST HEGEMONY?

In the aftermath of various setbacks in U.S. foreign policy—defeat in
the Vietnam War, the Iranian hostage episode, the energy crises of the
1970s, and chronic balance-of-payment deficits—many Americans are
inclined to believe in and bemoan the loss of U.S. hegemony in international affairs. The widespread feeling that U.S. influence has slipped
seriously accounts in part for the popularity of the hegemonic stability
theory, discussed in Chapter 4.

It is true that U.S. economic and military dominance over the rest of
the world was greater in the years immediately after World War II than
it is now, at the beginning of the 1990s. It is also true that Japan, West
Germany, the PRC, and the Soviet Union have improved their relative
economic and military position during the past forty-five years. Yet, the

U.S. world position in the late 1940s was quite peculiar: Whereas much of Europe and Asia had been devastated by war, North America was untouched by this destruction. Therefore, in comparison with the status of other major powers, U.S. supremacy stood out. At no other time in modern history has a country possessed such a commanding edge in military, economic, and technological power over its potential rivals as the United States did after World War II.

Although U.S. power has surely declined relatively since its peak in the late 1940s, in 1990 it is still much superior to that of its nearest competitors. For instance, although the USSR is generally believed to have achieved military parity with the United States, the latter still outspends Japan in defense by about twelve times and the PRC by fourteen times. The U.S. economy is still about twice as large as either the Japanese or the Soviet economy, four times larger than the West German economy, and ten times larger than the Chinese economy. Thus, whereas the relative dominance of the United States has slipped somewhat, its absolute superiority is still considerable.

One scholar has argued that "to be considered hegemonic in the world political economy . . . a country must have access to crucial raw materials, control major sources of capital, maintain a large market for imports, and hold comparative advantages in goods with high value added, yielding relatively high wages and profits. It must also be stronger, on these dimensions taken as a whole, than any other country."[1] According to these criteria, the United States is still the only country that qualifies as a hegemonic power in the capitalist world. It possesses a large base of natural resources. By comparison, Japan and West Germany are quite dependent on imports of raw materials from foreign sources, and both are much more vulnerable to a disruption of this supply. Concomitantly, the domestic Japanese and West German markets are much smaller than the U.S. market, and they are accordingly much more dependent on foreign sales than is the United States. Moreover, the United States still commands major sources of capital (the dollar remains the preferred currency for international trade and finance) and enjoys a competitive edge in advanced technologies, such as in aerospace and computers. Despite their recent export successes, the Japanese and the West Germans cannot match the U.S. advantages in raw materials, market size, capital assets, and technological lead. Although they may have narrowed the gap and even caught up in some respects (e.g., the Japanese in international financing and robotic technology), those countries cannot compete with the United States across the board. Actually, it is the *combined* U.S. superiority in the four areas just mentioned that gives it hegemonic power.

Another scholar has suggested four somewhat different aspects of **structural power**—that is, the power to determine the rules of international order:[2]

1. The ability to influence other people's physical security (through the exercise of military capabilities to threaten or defend this security)
2. The ability to control the global system of production of goods and services
3. The ability to determine the global system of international finance and credit
4. The ability to control and influence the development, accumulation, and transfer of knowledge—defined broadly to mean not only technology but also ideas and beliefs (fashion, fads, religion, ideology, intellectual trends)

Each of these four aspects of structural power supports the other three, and in combination, they provide the undergirding of a hegemon's international dominance. There is little question that neither Japan nor Western Europe currently has the necessary military capability to affect global security. They are far behind the United States on this dimension. Similarly, these countries lag behind the United States in "knowledge power" or cultural influence. One indication of this U.S. superiority is that the Nobel-prize winners in the natural sciences are disproportionately Americans. Another indication is that the United States is still the destination of choice for most foreign scholars and students, making U.S. campuses and research institutions the knowledge centers of the world.

With regard to the U.S. role in the global production of goods and services, there have indeed been some rather dramatic changes in the recent decades. The United States no longer has a comparative advantage in the manufacture of such products as shoes, textiles, television sets, and even steel and automobiles. However, these "sunset" industries are hardly at the cutting edge of technology. It is also true that increasingly the United States has found itself urging the capitalist East Asians to buy more U.S. beef, tobacco, wheat, cotton, and lumber. To that extent, there has been a role reversal. Contrary to the dependency perspective, the capitalist East Asians have now become the exporters of manufactures, while the United States (as well as Canada, Australia, and New Zealand) are relying more on the export of agricultural and mineral products. Therefore, a new division of labor seems to be emerging—the tables are now being turned on the United States, which had been accustomed to preaching the virtues of comparative advantage and free trade to the Third World.

Lest we conclude from this discussion and Washington's chronic trade deficits that the United States has lost its influence in the global system of production, we need to consider several points. First, in exercising structural power, the ownership and managerial control of production are more important than the location of production. In this respect, U.S.-owned and -managed multinational corporations are still predominant in the world of business. According to one account, about 250 of the world's largest multinational manufacturing and extractive firms are based in the United States, 150 in various Western European countries, 70 in Japan, and 20 in the rest of the world.[3] Thus, even though the sites of some industrial and manufacturing activities have shifted away from the United States, the ownership and managerial control of these activities have not changed hands.

Second, one strong and continuing comparative advantage enjoyed by the United States in trading with other countries is what economists call "invisibles." In contrast to commodities, which are visible, the invisibles constitute activities such as technology transfers, product design, management consulting, and financial and legal services. In fact, the control of technical know-how, product innovation, and investment capital is a more important element of structural power than the control of physical commodities.

Third, control of physical production and competitiveness in international trade are less important than superiority in military capabilities and command of international finance and credit.[4] To illustrate, although large deposits of petroleum are located in Middle Eastern countries (which have physical control over the production of this petroleum during normal times), the United States has the military power to destroy or seize this asset. To use another example, although Japan and West Germany may accumulate huge sums of U.S. dollars as a result of their trade surpluses, only Washington has the power to create and supply dollars—still the dominant currency for international payments.

The premier position of the U.S. dollar in turn gives Washington a dominant role in controlling the structure of international finance and credit. To finance its deficit in government spending and its deficit in foreign trade, Washington has in part been issuing more dollars. In doing so, it has been exporting its domestic inflation and forcing its trade partners to pay for its own extravagances. Only the United States enjoys the sort of unilateral freedom of action exemplified by its sudden decision in 1971 to abandon a long-standing commitment to convert the dollar into gold (thereby, in effect devaluing the dollar holdings of the U.S. trade partners). Referring to this incident, one scholar remarked:

In most countries, whether the balance-of-payments is in surplus or deficit indicates the strength or weakness of its financial position. With the United States, the exact converse can be true. Indeed, to run a persistent deficit for a quarter of a century with impunity indicates not American weakness, but rather American power in the system. To decide one August [1971] morning that dollars can no longer be converted into gold was a progression from exorbitant privilege to super-exorbitant privilege; the U.S. government was exercising the unconstrained right to print money that others could not (save at unacceptable cost) refuse to accept in payment.[5]

Therefore, there is a distinctly self-serving element in U.S. references to the country's being the principal provider of public goods and the insinuation that others have been free riders. Washington's manipulation of the dollar's value is reminiscent of the resort to overissuing and debasing coins by medieval rulers as a way of financing their extravagant consumption. The right of these rulers to issue legal tender and to profit from issuing it has been called the *seigniorage privilege*—a privilege that enables them to use inflation and currency devaluation to deal with their budgetary deficits. The burden of paying for this inflation and devaluation is passed on to the consumers, currency holders, and the exporters who sell to the "seignior" and who are paid with the debased money.

In the situation just described, we have private good for the hegemon and public bad for the followers (who get to pay for the hegemon's fiscal and monetary irresponsibilities). In Chapter 4, it was pointed out that the United States has persistently tried to have "guns" (high military expenditures) as well as "butter" (high welfare expenditures). At the same time, successive U.S. administrations have been reluctant to raise taxes to pay for these programs.[6] These tendencies to "get a quart out of a pint pot" have produced chronic and increasing budget deficits, inflationary pressure, and currency devaluation. Much of the costs for these "public bads" are transferred to and borne by the hegemon's trade partners. The fact that the United States has been able to force these costs onto others for so long is a sign of U.S. strength rather than weakness. In this light, the burgeoning trade surpluses and foreign currency reserves of Japan, West Germany, and other U.S. commercial partners are less consequential than the fact that "the United States is the only government capable of creating dollar assets that are accepted and saleable worldwide."[7] Being the world's treasurer (and thus having exclusive access to the printing press for money) does have some important private benefits. And for this as well as the other reasons mentioned above, talk of a vanishing U.S. hegemony is premature.

PAX CONSORTIS
OR REGIONAL BIGEMONY?

The theory of hegemonic stability implies that the demise of a hegemon will result in international disorder and chaos. This proposition, however, is doubtful. As we saw in Chapter 4, periods of hegemonic preponderance have not always been stable or peaceful; similarly, periods of a relative balance of power among the major countries have not always been accompanied by economic or military warfare. Indeed, there is some historical evidence that seems to contradict the hegemonic stability theory. Apparently, an equal distribution of power among several countries (as opposed to a preponderance of power enjoyed by a hegemon), changes toward greater power parity, and a fluid power hierarchy were associated with less war during the nineteenth century.[8] For the twentieth century, however, the evidence points in the opposite direction and is therefore more supportive of the hegemonic stability theory.

It seems that the presence of a hegemon is in itself neither a necessary nor a sufficient condition for international cooperation. Similarly, the absence of a hegemon does not automatically rule out the possibility of international cooperation. Governments have an important interest in creating norms and rules (called **regimes**) that enable those governments to have stable expectations and institutionalized procedures in acting together for joint gains (as in, for example, international trade and arms control). They also have a strong incentive to develop legal and moral conventions that discourage cheating, defection, or other kinds of unacceptable behavior in their relations with each other. These conventions— regarding the treatment of prisoners of war, the protection of civilians in warfare, the formal declaration of war, and the legal rights of neutral countries—are in the long-term interests of all members of the international community. They are often observed even by nations at war because it is in their mutual interest to abide by some rules and norms of military conduct. Thus, countries in military conflict frequently cooperate to establish and maintain procedural rules and behavioral norms.

Regimes may be occasionally inconvenient because they limit one's freedom of action and, indeed, may force one to act against one's immediate (myopic) interest in particular situations. However, regimes have the benefit of also imposing similar restraints on others. In this important sense, regimes are self-enforcing rather than necessarily dependent on an outside enforcer (such as a hegemon). To illustrate, the convention of traffic lights benefits all motorists. They stop at a red light, even though this convention can be a bit inconvenient occasionally (when one is in a big hurry to go somewhere or when there is little traffic in the middle of the night). However, these occasional inconveniences are far outweighed by the long-term benefits. The convention of traffic lights creates a common base of expectations and rules for mutual adjustment and is normally observed by motorists even when police enforcement is absent. In this sense, the convention is self-enforcing because motorists know that cheating (driving through an intersection when there is a red light) is detrimental to his or her long-term self-interest.

Accordingly, most observers do not expect hegemonic decline necessarily to bring in its wake international disorder and instability. Even in the absence of a hegemon to enforce rules and norms, government officials in different countries have a collective incentive in developing and institutionalizing regimes for international conduct. Thus, as one leading scholar on this topic has remarked, "Cooperation among independent governments in the absence of hegemony, to achieve joint gains, is possible, and . . . regimes can facilitate such cooperation by reducing transaction costs, providing information, and constructing rules of thumb to guide bureaucracies in making routine decisions."[9]

It is even possible that the decline of a hegemon can produce an international order that is collectively preferable to the one that the hegemon produced during the peak of its power.[10] To the extent that the relative decline of U.S. power is balanced by the relative rise of power of Japan and West Germany, the latter two now may have a greater incentive to see to it that certain public goods (international peace, monetary stability and liquidity, free movement of goods and capital) continue to be supplied. This is another way of saying that the rising status of Japan and West Germany gives them a greater stake in the international system, which in turn should diminish their incentive to free-ride, because of the fear that such behavior would undermine this system. Consequently, the gap left by the hegemon may very well be filled by a consortium of three powers (the United States, Japan, and West Germany). In this pact of domination by the "big three," the United States may be less able to impose its will on others than previously. However, saying this is quite different from suggesting that hegemonic decline will necessarily translate into less order, stability, or cooperation in world affairs.

Of course, if we restrict our attention to the capitalist Pacific area, we see that the influence of West Germany is rather limited. We are instead faced with the possible emergence of a **regional bigemony** (the rule of two hegemons). Although the United States continues to be the ultimate guarantor of the military security of this region, Japan has increasingly become the primary source of capital and technology for its neighbors as well as the major market for their exports of foodstuffs and raw materials. Japanese investment and technology have dominated the economies of Taiwan and South Korea (both former Japanese colonies), whereas Japanese imports have made Tokyo the biggest customer for the primary exports—such as petroleum (Indonesia), wheat and soybeans (Australia, Canada, the United States), lumber (Canada and the United States), and iron ore (Australia)—of its regional trade partners. At the same time, Japanese manufactures have established a dominant market position in practically all the Asian Pacific countries, including Thailand, Indonesia, the Philippines, Malaysia, South Korea, and Taiwan.

However, the United States continues to be the senior partner in the evolving regional bigemony. Besides holding the military key to the security and stability of this region, the United States also continues to be the primary knowledge center and export destination of the manufactures of the Pacific Rim countries. Moreover, Washington's military supremacy and its monetary power constitute two trump cards that can nullify Japanese advantages in other areas. To a significant extent, Japan will continue to rely in the near future on this U.S. power to ensure a steady supply of raw materials for its industries, open markets for its exports, stable political conditions in its trade partners, and regional and global peace so that its multinational corporations can invest and trade abroad.

SECURITY COMMUNITY AND FREE TRADE AREA?

It is quite remarkable that there has not been any major armed conflict among the capitalist Pacific Rim countries in the past forty-five years. During this period, these countries have developed an increasingly active and dense network of private as well as public ties that bind them together in an interdependent economic, political, and cultural system. These ties are manifested by the rising volume of trade flows, cross investments, interlocking financial deals, diplomatic consultation, cultural exchange, and tourism. At the same time, government officials, business leaders, and academic scholars have been gathering with increasing frequency in places like Canberra, Tokyo, Vancouver, and Manila to discuss problems of regional concern and to search for institutional frameworks for joint action.

To a limited extent, this situation is reminiscent of historical developments that had led to the formation of security communities in other areas. A **security community** is an area where people resolve their disputes through peaceful means. The idea of war among them has become unthinkable. In this sense, one can talk of a North Atlantic security community in which the resort to arms against another member of the community is no longer accepted.[11] Therefore, even though Britain,

France, and West Germany were once bitter enemies, they now do not prepare for war against one another. Similarly, the United States and Canada do not defend their common border because they do not expect military hostility from the other. Whereas difficulties among these neighbors do arise, the mutual expectation is that these difficulties will be resolved through hard negotiation rather than armed contest. Accordingly, ever since the end of World War II a "zone of peace"—a security community—has been maintained among the North American and Western European countries.

This security community has been buttressed by rising interaction (through trade, tourism, diplomatic visits) and cooperation (common defense against the USSR, coordination to defuse various monetary crises) among the people and officials of the North Atlantic area. It has also promoted the formation of common institutions for decision making, with the North Atlantic Treaty Organization and the European Economic Community (EEC, or the Common Market) being the most obvious examples. And for the Western Europeans, there has been an increase in a common European consciousness as opposed to exclusive national identification with individual countries, such as France, Italy, Belgium, or West Germany. The close political and economic cooperation among the Western Europeans will be given another push in 1992 when additional trade and immigration barriers separating their countries will be removed. Thus, Western Europe is poised to become a huge integrated area whose joint economic and political power will rival that of the two superpowers.

This economic and political integration of previously disparate entities has historical precedents. Successful economic cooperation based on the *Zollverein* (customs union) and rising German nationalism led to the formation of a unified Germany under the leadership of Prussia after Prussia defeated France in 1870. More familiar to Americans, increasing economic collaboration, cultural homogenization, and especially growth of a distinct American identity fostered a "we feeling" among the settlers of the thirteen original colonies and eventually led to their demand for an independent political union.[12]

In the near future, comparable developments are not likely in the Pacific region. Although the capitalist countries in this area no longer guard against military attack from one another, it is still premature to imagine the sort of economic and political integration that has taken place in Western Europe since the 1950s. This prognosis does not dismiss important ongoing efforts by interested academics, businesspeople, and former officials of the Pacific Rim countries to launch various cooperative arrangements (the most recent example being the meeting on Asia Pacific Economic Cooperation, held in November 1989 at Canberra, Australia).

However, several issues undermine the prospect of this integration in the Pacific context.

First, the countries in this region have a more diverse cultural background and more uneven economic development than those that obtain in Western Europe or North America. A regional consciousness does not currently exist; and because of the great disparities in industrial maturity, fears of economic exploitation and domination abound. Second, just as there are still widespread concerns in Western Europe about a resurgent (and, in view of recent events, a reunified) Germany, Japan's Asian neighbors have not forgotten Tokyo's military exploits in World War II. Those memories are still vivid in the minds of many leaders, who obviously do not welcome Japan's renewed domination (even if based on economic power rather than military force) in a new regional order. Third, Beijing and Moscow are skeptical of any regional arrangement that excludes the socialist countries. They fear that such regional arrangements may be disguised political or military coalitions that the capitalist countries are organizing against them. Finally, the United States is not currently interested in any multilateral agreement for a free trade area. It suspects that proposals for such an agreement are merely an attempt by the East Asian exporting countries to assure themselves of continued access to the U.S. consumer market. Washington prefers instead to maintain its bargaining leverage and flexibility through bilateral negotiations with its East Asian trade partners.

On a smaller scale, the six members of the Association of Southeast Asian Nations (ASEAN) have undertaken collaborative efforts to pursue their joint concerns.[13] Launched in 1967, this regional organization had the declared purpose of enhancing the economic, social, and cultural cooperation among its member states (originally, Indonesia, Malaysia, the Philippines, Singapore, and Thailand, later joined by Brunei). During its earlier years, ASEAN deliberately deemphasized the goals of political and military collaboration in order to avoid exacerbating the existing differences of view among the member states and in order to deflect the apprehension and opposition of other countries (most particularly Vietnam and the PRC).

In subsequent years, however, ASEAN's greatest achievements were in instituting mechanisms of diplomatic consultation, including a regular series of meetings among the member states' top officials. It played a particularly active role in mediating the ongoing conflict in Cambodia. However, despite its professed desire to develop industrial complementarity and to expand bilateral trade among its member states, the actual level of economic interaction among its members has been quite low (except in the case of Singapore and Malaysia). Moreover, except for Singapore, the member countries rely heavily on the export of primary goods (e.g., tin, rubber, palm oil, petroleum), which sometimes puts them in a competitive trade relationship. Japan is much more important for the ASEAN states' economies (either as a buyer of their exports or as a supplier of their imports) than the states are to each other. At the same time, there have been few cultural exchanges among these countries that would promote a common regional identification. Thus, unlike the European and U.S. cases, ASEAN has been primarily motivated by government initiatives to enhance diplomatic coordination. These efforts, however, have not given comparable attention to promoting common economic interests and cultural concerns that are necessary to sustain the integration process.

In short, then, although the spirit of Thomas Hobbes has clearly abated among the capitalist East Asian countries (and since the 1970s, between them and some socialist countries), the spirit of Camelot is still hardly visible. Political or economic integration is unlikely to produce major changes in the regional structure in the foreseeable future. Nevertheless, one can expect continued close political consultation and economic collaboration among the Pacific Rim countries, meaning that a return to the days of cold war is also improbable.

COMPLEX INTERDEPENDENCE

The current and most likely (at least in the short-term) future situation applying to the Pacific Basin may be best described as **complex interdependence.** This term was originally developed by two authors to show the dawning of a new era in international affairs.[14] The era of complex interdependence is characterized by several features.

First, there is a relative decline in the salience of military capabilities. As a result of both the massive destructive power of modern weapons and the strategic stalemate between the two superpowers, the officials of leading states are increasingly self-deterred from the use of armed forces (at least against each other). At the same time, national possession of instruments of military assertion—tanks, planes, and battleships— has become less determinative than in the past of international status. Consequently, even though Japan and West Germany lack a military capability for overseas deployment or strategic deterrence, they are nevertheless important international actors because of their economic power. Another sign of the declining salience of military capabilities in an era of complex interdependence is that it has become increasingly difficult for countries to use their military influence to achieve bargaining gains in other issue areas (such as in trade and monetary negotiations). This does not mean that armed forces are no longer relevant to world politics, for they remain important instruments of statecraft and an indispensable aspect of a country's structural power. Rather, with the onset of complex interdependence, military capabilities tend to be assigned to the backstage of state interactions. The overt resort to arms or military displays has become unpopular as well as imprudent in the age of nuclear weapons.

Second, complex interdependence is characterized by the emergence of "nontraditional" issues and actors in international relations. The traditional concerns of statecraft—defense of territorial integrity, deterrence against foreign aggression, and formation of military alliances—lose some of their urgency because of the nuclear balance between the two superpowers and the military protection each extends to its allies. In their place, nontraditional issues—such as the management of international monetary stability, the maintenance of a liberal trade order, the regulation of foreign direct investment, and the preservation of earth's ecology—demand increasing attention from policymakers. And with the rising salience of these issues, nontraditional actors—such as international banks, multinational corporations, intergovernmental cartels (e.g., the Organization of Petroleum Exporting Countries), transnational groups (e.g., Amnesty International, Greenpeace)—have become more active participants in international relations.

Third and as a result of the first two, the tapestry of international relations has become more intricate. Multiple and changing issues crowd the policymakers' agenda, and national and transnational participants form shifting coalitions across different issues. Thus, an ally on one issue today may be a rival on another issue tomorrow. The hierarchy of issues and the demarcation of friends and foes have become more fluid and uncertain. At the same time, there will be greater mobility, up or down, in the international hierarchy. Some countries will suffer a relative decline in national power or international status, while others will experience a relative ascendance. The status rankings and movements need not be concordant (e.g., Japan may be an economic superpower but a military dependent), so that discrepancy between different dimensions of power is more common than harmony between them in the age of complex interdependence.

Finally, the distinction between domestic politics and economics on the one hand, and foreign politics and economics on the other, becomes blurred. Events in the domestic arena tend to have ripple effects internationally, just as foreign developments are likely to have domestic consequences. For instance, domestic inflation can undermine export competitiveness, whereas the penetration of foreign goods into the domestic market can exacerbate domestic unemployment. In a world where countries' relations with one another are marked by frequent and multiple contacts, it is increasingly difficult to separate the arenas for domestic and foreign policies.

As we enter the final decade of the twentieth century, we can see that the Pacific region has undergone a period of relative military détente. In 1989 the Vietnamese pulled their troops out of Cambodia, thus lowering the tension level between Hanoi and Beijing. The visit by Soviet leader Mikhail Gorbachev to the PRC, also in 1989, similarly led to a mutual military deescalation along the borders of these two Communist giants. Additionally, the military tension between North and South Korea, and between the PRC and Taiwan, has abated considerably in recent years. Consequently, military issues and concerns seem no longer to occupy a priority position in the policy agendas of most Pacific Rim countries.

Instead, concerns with economic development, export competitiveness, resource supply, market access, foreign investment, and technology transfers have assumed greater importance in the minds of officials. Indeed, even the general public seems to agree that we have left the cold war era of military containment and ideological rivalry and have entered a new period of industrial transformation and trade competition. Thus, the August 1989 issue of *Business Week* reported that, by a margin of three to one, Americans were more concerned with Japan's economic competition than with the Soviet Union's military threat.

In this light, some previous protectorates of the United States—Japan, Taiwan, and South Korea—are increasingly being perceived as commercial rivals. In contrast, the PRC—once an enemy—is being seen as a potentially huge market for U.S. products and investment as well as a strategic counterbalance to Soviet influence. Similarly, as a result of the rising protectionist sentiments in the United States and chronic instability in their resource suppliers, Japan and South Korea are beginning to cast glances at the PRC and the USSR as potential export markets and as sources of raw materials for their manufactures and industries. Finally, the Chinese and the Soviets have shown increasing signs of willingness to turn to Japan and the United States as a potential source of foreign capital and technology to aid their respective economic modernization.

Accordingly, the relations among these countries have become more complex and less symmetrical. They may cooperate on some issues, such as the preservation of the status quo on the Korean peninsula and the prevention of another war between the rival regimes there. They may, however, compete fiercely for commercial or strategic advantages elsewhere. Thus, for example, the United States and Japan have kept a keen eye on each other in order to prevent the other country from achieving a dominant position in the Chinese market. Similarly, competition among

Japanese, Taiwanese, and South Korean exporters and investors has become more intense in the United States as well as in Southeast Asia.

Yet in the final analysis, this competition has to be understood in a broader context of cooperation. Simply put, the capitalist East Asian countries need the United States for its military protection and its consumer market. Conversely, the United States wants the cooperation of these countries to block any Soviet expansion and to avoid economic disruptions. Finally, Washington, Moscow, Beijing, and Tokyo need each other to ensure and sustain peace and order in the region. For these reasons, complex interdependence seems to describe well the ongoing and near-term relations among the Pacific Rim countries.

LONG CYCLE AND *PAX NIPPONICA?*

Several scholars, when they step back and take a longer-term view of the history of the international political economy, have noticed some regular patterns in the rise and decline of nations. Although they disagree about the specific timing and duration of power transition, they have commented that changes in world affairs seem to have come in waves or cycles of several decades.

One such scholar has developed the idea of **long cycles** to describe the ebb and flow of international power and the occurrence of great wars.[15] He has noted that there have been five "long cycles" since 1494, each period lasting about one century. These cycles were (1) 1494–1580, under Portuguese leadership; (2) 1580–1688, under Dutch leadership; (3) 1688–1792, under the first British leadership; (4) 1792–1914, under the second British leadership; and (5) from 1914 until about the end of the twentieth century, under U.S. leadership.

The five long cycles were each divided into four stages: (1) great war, (2) the rise of a global leader, (3) delegitimation of power, and (4) deconcentration of power. A major war involving many countries has historically paved the way for the emergence of a new hegemon. This new global leader has not necessarily had to be the one with the largest army or the biggest economy; instead, global leaders in the past were the greatest naval powers of their era (Portugal, the Netherlands, Britain). At the same time, the new global leader had been an ally rather than a rival of the previous global leader (Britain was a Dutch ally, and the United States was a British ally). The challenger to the global leader (e.g., imperial Spain and Germany) typically initiated a great war that it could not win. However, the global leader was seriously weakened by this assault, and the baton of leadership was passed on to its major ally (who became the new global leader).

Each long cycle followed a pattern of rising and then falling international order. The opening period of global war was a time of intense economic and especially military struggle (the Napoleonic War in the early 1800s, World War I in the second decade of the twentieth century). It was a period of turmoil and uncertainty. This was followed by the termination of the great war and the emergence of a new global leader, or hegemon. Order was reestablished in this period. However, with the passage of time the legitimacy of the global leader came under increasing scrutiny and challenge in the next period. Finally, the global leader underwent a relative power decline in the final period, so that it could no longer impose international order. Its leadership came under attack by challengers who had increased their relative power. This deconcentration of power in the international system led to the breakdown of order and stability and ushered in a period of great war—thereby initiating the next cycle of global political economy.

There seems to be some association between the leadership cycles and world economic cycles. One formulation suggests that periods of great war and power delegitimation (periods 1 and 3 above) also tend to be periods of rising inflation, technological stagnation, and international competition for resources. In contrast, periods characterized by the rise of a global leader (period 2 above) and the subsequent deconcentration of its power (period 4 above) appear to be associated with technological innovation, resource abundance, and relative economic prosperity. According to this view, economic prosperity seems to precipitate or accompany the relative decline of the global leader and to usher in the subsequent period of military strife and great war.

In Chapter 4, we observed that rapid economic growth can be destabilizing domestically. We now speculate that it may also upset the existing international order. Economic dynamism and expansion may be precursors of subsequent rivalry and warfare among the major powers for several reasons. First, changing comparative advantage and technological breakthrough enable the follower countries to close the gap between themselves and the global leader. Second, rapid economic growth, especially when combined with rising domestic population pressure, impels leaders to look for foreign colonies, markets, and sources of raw materials. If several countries are under the same **lateral pressure** (a tendency toward foreign expansion and international rivalry that occurs when countries experience rapid economic and population growth) to seek territorial and economic expansion, they are launched on a collision course that often ends in war.[16] The competition between Britain and Germany for African colonies prior to World War I and the rivalry between Japan and the United States for economic and political dominance in the Pacific before World War II offer historical illustrations of this process leading to war. Third, economic prosperity may increase the danger of war because it makes armament expenditures more affordable and influences leaders to be more aggressive and self-confident in their foreign policies.[17]

Accordingly, the recent economic dynamism and expansion of the capitalist East Asian countries *may* suggest a greater danger of warfare and military competition in the years ahead (during the early decades of the twenty-first century?). Already we have noticed a relative—not absolute—decline in U.S. power, especially in the realm of international trade and productivity. Concomitantly, there has been a tendency toward power deconcentration in the world, so that the distance separating U.S. capabilities and those of the other major powers (Japan, West Germany, the USSR, and the PRC) is narrower today than, say, four decades ago. Finally, trade frictions, protectionist sentiments, monetary instability, and competition for markets and raw materials have clearly been on the rise in recent years. These developments may encourage or exacerbate rivalry among the leading contenders in their race to become the next hegemon.

What can we infer from history about those attributes that a successful global hegemon is likely to have? The leading proponent of the long cycle theory offers the following four "factors of world leadership"[18]:

1. A favorable geography, preferably an island nation
2. A socially cohesive and politically open domestic system
3. A dynamic economy that is the world's leader
4. A political and strategic organization that provides for "global reach"

Historically, an insular location has tended to discourage foreign invasion and to promote seafaring capabilities. Insularity has also facilitated a more homogeneous and cohesive society (in language, ethnicity, and religion), which in turn has promoted more stable and perhaps open politics. The global leader does not necessarily have the largest economy in absolute size, but it does have the advantages of possessing the most dynamic entrepreneurs, the most innovative technologies, and the strongest commercial and financial establishments of its day. Finally, it has the political and strategic organization to project its influence on a global scale. In previous eras, this meant the possession of a dominant naval force, although in the next cycle air and perhaps even space power would have to be taken into account.

The long cycle theory does not predict who will become the next global leader. However, the case of Japan does come to mind, given the preceding enumeration of the qualifying or facilitating characteristics of a hegemonic leader. Japan is an island nation that has a homogeneous culture and population. It also has an open and efficient political system. It has some of the largest and most productive industries, trading companies, and banking groups in the world. Close collaboration between the public and private sectors and constant industrial adjustment and adaptation have produced a very dynamic economy, which is outward rather than inward looking. Although Japan is not quite a world technology leader in all or even most areas, it has demonstrated an ample capacity to keep up and even catch up (in robotics, semiconductors, biogenetics, aerospace). Finally, it does have a large merchant fleet as befitting its seafaring tradition, although it currently lags behind the United States and the USSR in air and space power.

The scenario just sketched may sound implausible to some readers but convincing and even alarming to others. One must admit that we social scientists have not generally been very good at making forecasts. The farther we try to look into the future, the cloudier our crystal ball gets. The preceding discussion about long cycles and Japan's future role in the world's political economy is intended to be argumentative rather than indicative. It is especially important to mention three caveats in regard to this discussion.

First, history is useful for illustrating alternative developmental possibilities. It does not necessarily unfold mechanically according to some preordained steps. Thus, despite the oft-heard statement about history repeating itself, it is likely that the future will not duplicate the past. The preceding discussion should thus be seen as an attempt to introduce some historical knowledge to inform our thinking about alternative futures, rather than as an invitation to extrapolate the future mechanically from the past.

Second, although power transitions in the past seem to have been accompanied by devastating warfare and political turmoil, that does not mean that the next cycle will also be initiated by a global war. Given the destructive power of modern weapons, the next global war may very well mean the end of human civilization. Therefore, there should be a strong collective incentive to develop a procedure for leadership transfer other than through resort to arms. If the human race is unsuccessful in developing this alternative procedure, it may not survive and the next long cycle will hardly matter.

Finally, I argued earlier in this book that with the onset of complex interdependence, the traditional tools and preoccupations of statecraft have become less appropriate or relevant in the normal conduct of international relations. Indeed, in the period after World War II, those countries that have adopted a "trading strategy" have tended to outperform others that continue to give primacy to the ideas of military assertiveness and territorial control.[19] Accordingly, the resort to arms becomes increasingly an inefficient as well as an imprudent approach to engineering upward mobility in the international system. Future power transitions and leadership transfers, therefore, do not necessarily have to be decided by military contests.

CONCLUSION

History, comparative politics, and international political economy have tended to exist as separate fields of scholarship. In this volume, I tried to bring together some strands of recent scholarly inquiry in these fields in order to offer some explanations as well as implications of East Asian dynamism. I compared the experiences and practices of the countries in this area with their counterparts in other parts of the Pacific region. I also suggested some alternative theoretical perspectives that attempt to account for the divergent experiences and practices of those countries.

The values of economic growth, sociopolitical order, and military and resource security are widely shared by the masses and officials of different countries. However, controversies abound regarding the most efficacious ways to attain these goals. In the preceding discussions, I tried to provide a sense of the variety of opinions and views on this subject and to show the complexity of issues involved. This complexity results from the interactions and side effects of the values of growth, order, and security. In many situations, officials are faced with policy dilemmas because the pursuit of one value may undermine the achievement of another. At the same time, domestic performances with respect to these values often have important ramifications for foreign policy successes or failures, just as foreign conditions and achievements affect domestic performances. Thus there is a close interaction between domestic political economy on the one hand and international political economy on the other. The challenge to wise and prudent policymaking stems from the necessity to choose among contending theories, to adjust to possible value trade-offs, and to manage simultaneously the domestic and foreign arenas—the three constant sources of policy dilemma.

For readers who are sufficiently intrigued by this book's topical treatment, there is a reference section, "Suggested Readings." The glossary presents short definitions of important concepts discussed in this book.

□   □   □

Discussion Questions

CHAPTER ONE

1. What are the major currents in recent world history? How are these trends and developments likely to affect the future of the global political economy?

2. What do you foresee to be the role of the Pacific region in the evolving global political economy as we enter the twenty-first century?

CHAPTER TWO

1. What does the concept of world system mean? How did this world system emerge historically, and how was the Pacific region incorporated into this system?

2. Why was Meiji Japan more successful in pursuing economic modernization than was Qing China? What were the major domestic and foreign factors affecting the developmental histories of these two countries during the century before World War II?

3. What in your view have been the most important goals of U.S. officials in their policies toward East Asia in this century? Have these policies been motivated primarily by economic interests, military concerns, or ideological preoccupation? How successful has Washington been in containing the influence of economic, military, or ideological rivals in the Pacific region?

CHAPTER THREE

1. Should countries pursue their comparative advantage in economic policy, or should they emphasize national autonomy and self-sufficiency? What are the arguments in favor or against these divergent emphases? How are these arguments germane to the choice between export expansion and import substitution as a national strategy for economic modernization?

2. Would you favor a greater role for the market or for the government in domestic as well as international economics? Why? In view of the growing U.S. trade deficits, would you favor more governmental intervention to limit foreign imports and to protect domestic jobs? And in view of the recent political turmoil in the PRC, would you advise that country's leaders to continue its economic liberalization and to reduce further the role of government planning and subsidy? Are your answers to these questions consistent?

3. What are the main differences between U.S. and Japanese officials' definitions and conceptualizations of national security? In what ways have these differences been influenced by the divergent historical experiences and national endowments of these two countries? Do you see any need for major adjustments in Washington's and Tokyo's images of their respective national security in light of recent developments in the world?

CHAPTER FOUR

1. Why do some scholars expect rapid economic growth to engender social frustration, exacerbate income inequality, and increase the danger of political instability? Why do other analysts argue the converse, that social tranquility, political stability, and electoral politics based on the rivalry among many interest groups can in the long run produce economic stagnation and social rigidity? Do you see any way out of the policy dilemmas posed by these hypotheses?

2. In what ways may military defeat in past wars and defense spending to prevent future wars affect national economic performance? What tentative conclusions can we draw about these effects from the Pacific context? Do you think Japan has been a "free rider" in the provision of collective defense for the capitalist countries? Do you believe that the United States should push Japan to spend more on this collective defense?

3. What are the chief arguments of the so-called hegemonic stability theory? How applicable is this theory to recent developments affecting the U.S. role in international affairs? Do the predictions of this theory point to more discord and chaos or to more harmony and cooperation in the international system as we approach the twenty-first century?

CHAPTER FIVE

1. On balance, do you believe "persistent dominance" or "lost hegemony" characterizes more accurately the current and immediate future role of the United States in the world political economy? Why? To what extent does the United States still enjoy and to what extent is it likely to continue to enjoy control of the key leverages of international structural power?

2. What do you see as the most probable direction of evolution for the Pacific region? Do you see any signs of a developing security community, emerging rival trade blocs, or deepening complex interdependence? Alternatively, do you believe that the world is poised to enter another long cycle, and, if you do, how do you expect the leadership transition to take place?

□ □ □

Notes

CHAPTER TWO

1. L. W. Pye, *China: An Introduction* (Boston: Little, Brown, 1984), p. 111.

2. I. Wallerstein, *The Modern World-System: Capitalist Agriculture and the Origins of the European World-Economy in the Sixteenth Century* (New York: Academic Press, 1974), p. 57.

3. K. A. Rasler and W. R. Thompson, "War-Making and State-Making: Governmental Expenditures, Tax Revenues, and Global War," *American Political Science Review* 79 (1985): 491–507.

4. M. Weber, *The Religion of China* (New York: Macmillan, 1964), pp. 103–104.

5. M. J. Levy, Jr., "Contrasting Factors in the Modernization of China and Japan," *Economic Development and Cultural Change* 2 (1953–54): 161–197.

6. F. V. Moulder, *Japan, China and the Modern World Economy* (New York: Cambridge University Press, 1979), p. 99.

7. Ibid., p. 191.

8. Pye, *China: An Introduction*, p. 117.

9. Moulder, *Japan, China and the Modern World Economy*, pp. 92, 184.

10. B. M. Russett, "Refining Deterrence Theory: The Japanese Attack on Pearl Harbor," p. 134 in D. G. Pruitt and R. C. Snyder (eds.), *Theory and Research on the Causes of War* (Englewood Cliffs, N.J.: Prentice-Hall, 1969).

11. B. Cumings, "The Origin and Development of the Northeast Asian Political Economy: Industrial Sectors, Product Cycle, and Political Consequences," *International Organization* 38 (1984): 24.

12. D. Ellsberg, "The Quagmire Theory and the Stalemate Machine," *Public Policy* 19 (1971): 217–274.

13. D. Zagoria, *The Vietnam Triangle* (New York: Pegasus, 1967).

14. Quoted in P. McMichael, "Foundations of U.S./Japanese World-Economic Rivalry in the 'Pacific Rim,'" *Journal of Developing Societies* 3 (1987): 65.

CHAPTER THREE

1. D. Ricardo, *Principles of Political Economy and Taxation* (London: Dent, 1933).

2. M. Friedman and R. Friedman, *Free to Choose* (New York: Harcourt, Brace, Jovanovich, 1980).

3. B. Balassa, *The Newly Industrializing Countries in the World Economy* (New York: Pergamon, 1981), p. 15.

4. H. Harding, *China's Second Revolution: Reform After Mao* (Washington, D.C.: The Brookings Institution, 1987), pp. 108–109.

5. Ibid., p. 293.

6. C. Johnson, *MITI and the Japanese Miracle* (Stanford, Calif.: Stanford University Press, 1982), pp. 18–21.

7. Ibid., p. 19.

8. T. J. Pempel, "Japanese Foreign Economic Policy: The Domestic Bases for International Behavior," pp. 139–190 in P. J. Katzenstein (ed.), *Between Power and Plenty* (Madison: University of Wisconsin Press, 1978).

9. D. B. Yoffie, *Power and Protectionism: Strategies of the Newly Industrializing Countries* (New York: Columbia University Press, 1983).

10. S. Reich, "Roads to Follow: Regulating Direct Foreign Investment," *International Organization* 43 (1989): 573.

11. D. Friedman, *The Misunderstood Miracle: Industrial Development and Political Change in Japan* (Ithaca, N.Y.: Cornell University Press, 1988).

12. D. Morawetz, *Why the Emperor's Clothes Are Not Made in Colombia?* (London: Oxford University Press, 1981).

13. The idea of asymmetric attention was discussed by A. O. Hirschman, *National Power and the Structure of Foreign Trade* (Berkeley: University of California Press, 1945).

14. V. Bornschier and C. Chase-Dunn, *Transnational Corporations and Under-development* (New York: Praeger, 1985).

15. C. Huang, "The State and Foreign Investment: The Cases of Taiwan and Singapore," *Comparative Political Studies* 22 (1989): 93–121.

16. Discussions on these topics can be found in F. C. Deyo, "Labor and Development Policy in East Asia," pp. 152–161 in P. A. Gourevitch (ed.), *The Pacific Region: Challenges to Policy and Theory* (Newbury Park, Calif.: Sage, 1989); P. Evans, "Class, State, and Dependence in East Asia: Lessons for Latin Americanists," pp. 203–226 in F. C. Deyo (ed.), *The Political Economy of the New Asian Industrialism* (Ithaca, N.Y.: Cornell University Press, 1987); and S. Haggard, "The Newly Industrializing Countries in the International System," *World Politics* 38 (1986): 343–370.

17. D. B. Bobrow and R. T. Kudrle, "How Middle Powers Can Manage Resource Weakness: Japan and Energy," *World Politics* 39 (1987): 536–565.

18. R. J. Samuels, "Consuming for Production: Japanese National Security, Nuclear Fuel Procurement, and the Domestic Economy," *International Organization* 43 (1989): 628.

19. See Mark A. Boyer, "Trading Public Goods in the Western Alliance System," *Journal of Conflict Resolution* 33 (1989): 700–727.

CHAPTER FOUR

1. See, for example, H. Kahn, "The Confucian Ethic and Economic Growth," pp. 78–80 in M. A. Seligson (ed.), *The Gap Between the Rich and Poor* (Boulder, Colo.: Westview Press, 1984).

2. S. M. Lipset, "Some Social Requisites of Democracy: Economic Development and Political Legitimacy," *American Political Science Review* 53 (1959): 69–105.

3. M. Olson, Jr., "Rapid Growth As A Destabilizing Force," *Journal of Economic History* 23 (1963): 536.

4. T. R. Gurr, *Why Men Rebel* (Princeton, N.J.: Princeton University Press, 1970).

5. A. de Tocqueville, *L'Ancien Régime*, trans. M. W. Patterson (Oxford: Basil Blackwell, 1947), p. 106.

6. M. Olson, Jr., *The Rise and Decline of Nations* (New Haven, Conn.: Yale University Press, 1982).

7. N. R. Miller, "Pluralism and Social Choice," *American Political Science Review* 77 (1983): 734–747.

8. World Bank, *World Development Report 1988* (New York: Oxford University Press, 1988), p. 223.

9. S. Chan, "Growth with Equity: A Test of Olson's Theory for the Asian Pacific-Rim Countries," *Journal of Peace Research* 24 (1987): 135–149.

10. World Bank, *World Development Report 1988*, p. 273.

11. S. Kuznets, "Economic Growth and Income Inequality," *American Economic Review* 45 (1955): 1–28.

12. For a review of the pertinent literature, see S. Chan, "The Impact of Defense Spending on Economic Performance: A Survey of Evidence and Problems," *ORBIS* 29 (1985): 403–434.

13. B. M. Russett, "Defense Expenditures and National Well-Being," *American Political Science Review* 76 (1982): 767–777.

14. A. S. Whiting, *Siberian Development and East Asia: Threat or Promise?* (Stanford, Calif.: Stanford University Press, 1981).

15. The proposition of uneven distribution of alliance burden was originally formulated by M. Olson, Jr., and R. Zeckhauser, "An Economic Theory of Alliances," *Review of Economics and Statistics* 48 (1966): 266–279. For two empirical tests of this proposition, see B. M. Russett, *What Price Vigilance? The Burdens of National Defense* (New Haven, Conn.: Yale University Press, 1970); and H. Starr, "A Collective Goods Analysis of Warsaw Pact After Czechoslovakia," *International Organization* 28 (1974): 521–532.

16. Discussions relating to this topic can be found in the following works: C. P. Kindleberger, "Dominance and Leadership in the International Economy," *International Studies Quarterly* 25 (1981): 242–254, and *The World in Depression, 1929–1939* (Berkeley: University of California Press, 1973); S. D. Krasner, "State Power and the Structure of International Trade," *World Politics* 28 (1976): 317–347; and A. A. Stein, "The Hegemon's Dilemma: Great Britain, the United States, and the International Economic Order," *International Organization* 38 (1984): 355–386.

17. J. D. Singer, S. Bremer, and J. Stuckey, "Capability Distribution, Uncertainty, and Major Power War, 1820–1965," pp. 19–48 in B. M. Russett (ed.), *Peace, War, and Numbers* (Beverly Hills, Calif.: Sage, 1972).

18. A.F.K. Organski, *World Politics* (New York: Knopf, 1958); and A.F.K. Organski and J. Kugler, *The War Ledger* (Chicago: University of Chicago Press, 1980).

19. B. M. Russett, "The Mysterious Case of Vanishing Hegemony: Or, Is Mark Twain Really Dead?" *International Organization* 39 (1985): 207–232.

20. Ibid., p. 218.

21. Ibid., p. 231.

CHAPTER FIVE

1. R. O. Keohane, *After Hegemony: Cooperation and Discord in the World Political Economy* (Princeton, N.J.: Princeton University Press, 1984), pp. 33–34.

2. S. Strange, "The Persistent Myth of Lost Hegemony," *International Organization* 41 (1987): 565.

3. R. Vernon, *Storm Over the Multinationals: The Real Issues* (Cambridge, Mass.: Harvard University Press, 1977), p. 12.

4. Strange, "The Persistent Myth of Lost Hegemony."

5. Ibid., pp. 568–569.

6. D. Calleo, *The Imperious Economy* (Cambridge, Mass.: Harvard University Press, 1982).

7. Strange, "The Persistent Myth of Lost Hegemony," p. 568.

8. J. D. Singer, S. Bremer, and J. Stuckey, "Capability Distribution, Uncertainty, and Major Power War, 1820–1965," pp. 19–48 in B. M. Russett (ed.), *Peace, War, and Numbers* (Beverly Hills, Calif.: Sage, 1972).

9. Keohane, *After Hegemony*, p. 221.

10. D. Snidal, "The Limits of Hegemonic Stability Theory," *International Organization* 37 (1985): 579–614.

11. K. W. Deutsch et al., *Political Community and the North Atlantic Area: International Organization in the Light of Historical Experience* (New York: Greenwood, 1957).

12. R. Merritt, *Symbols of American Community* (New Haven, Conn.: Yale University Press, 1966).

13. S. Chan, "The Association of Southeast Asian Nations: Some Indications on Regional Integration," *Tamkang Area Studies Journal* 7 (1986): 83–94; and S. W. Simon, "The ASEAN States: Obstacles to Security Cooperation," *ORBIS* 22 (1978): 415–434.

14. R. O. Keohane and J. S. Nye, *Power and Interdependence: World Politics in Transition* (Boston: Little, Brown, 1977).

15. G. Modelski, *Long Cycles in World Politics* (Seattle: University of Washington Press, 1987), and G. Modelski (ed.), *Exploring Long Cycles* (Boulder, Colo.: Lynne Rienner, 1987).

16. N. Choucri and R. C. North, *Nations in Conflict: National Growth and International Violence* (San Francisco: W. H. Freeman, 1975).

17. J. Goldstein, "Kondrateiff Waves as War Cycles," *International Studies Quarterly* 29 (1985): 411–441.

18. Modelski, *Exploring Long Cycles*, pp. 142–143.

19. R. Rosecrance, *The Rise of the Trading State: Commerce and Conquest in the Modern World* (New York: Basic Books, 1986).

□ □ □

Suggested Readings

Aggarwal, V. K., R. O. Keohane, and D. B. Yoffie. "The Dynamics of Negotiated Protectionism." *American Political Science Review* 81 (1987): 345–366.

Balassa, B. *The Newly Industrializing Countries in the World Economy.* New York: Pergamon, 1981.

Bobrow, D. B., and S. Chan. "Assets, Liabilities, and Strategic Conduct: Status Management by Japan, Taiwan, and South Korea." *Pacific Focus* 1 (1986): 23–56.

Bobrow, D. B., and R. T. Kudrle. "How Middle Powers Can Manage Resource Weakness: Japan and Energy." *World Politics* 39 (1987): 536–565.

Bornschier, V., and C. Chase-Dunn. *Transnational Corporations and Underdevelopment.* New York: Praeger, 1985.

Boyer, M. A. "Trading Public Goods in the Western Alliance System." *Journal of Conflict Resolution* 33 (1989): 700–727.

Caporaso, J. A. "Industrialization in the Periphery: The Evolving Global Division of Labor." *International Studies Quarterly* 25 (1981): 347–384.

Chan, S. "Growth with Equity: A Test of Olson's Theory for the Asian Pacific-Rim Countries." *Journal of Peace Research* 24: (1987): 135–149.

_____ . "The Mouse That Roared: Taiwan's Management of Trade Relations with the U.S." *Comparative Political Studies* 20 (1987): 251–292.

_____ . "The Impact of Defense Spending on Economic Performance: A Survey of Evidence and Problems." *ORBIS* 29 (1985): 403–434.

_____ . "Cores and Peripheries: Interaction Patterns in Asia." *Comparative Political Studies* 15 (1982): 314–340.

Chen, P.J.S. (ed.). *Singapore Development Policies and Trends.* Singapore: Oxford University Press, 1983.

Choucri, N., and R. C. North. *Nations in Conflict: National Growth and International Violence.* San Francisco: W. H. Freeman, 1975.

Chu, Y. H. "State Structure and Economic Adjustment of the East Asian Newly Industrializing Countries." *International Organization* 43 (1989): 647–672.

Clark, C. "The Taiwan Exception: Implications for Contending Political Economy Paradigms." *International Studies Quarterly* 31 (1987): 327–356.

Clark, C., and S. Chan (eds.). "The East Asian Development Model." *International Studies Notes,* special issue (1990).

Clark, C., and J. Lemco (eds.). *State and Development.* Leiden, Netherlands: Brill, 1988.

Cumings, B. "The Origin and Development of the Northeast Asian Political Economy: Industrial Sectors, Product Cycles, and Political Consequences." *International Organization* 38 (1984): 1–40.

———. *The Origins of the Korean War: Liberation and the Emergence of Separate Regimes*. Princeton, N.J.: Princeton University Press, 1981.

Deutsch, K. W., S. A. Burrell, R. A. Kann, M. Lee, Jr., M. Lichtenman, R. E. Lindgren, F. L. Loewenheim, and R. W. Van Wagenen. *Political Community and the North Atlantic Area: International Organization in the Light of Historical Experience*. New York: Greenwood, 1957.

Deyo, F. C. "Labor and Development Policy in East Asia." Pp. 152–161 in *The Pacific Region: Challenges to Policy and Theory*, edited by P.A. Gourevitch. Newbury Park, Calif.: Sage, 1989.

———. *Dependent Development and Industrial Order: An Asian Case Study*. New York: Praeger, 1981.

——— (ed.). *The Political Economy of the New Asian Industrialism*. Ithaca, N.Y.: Cornell University Press, 1987.

Ellsberg, D. "The Quagmire Myth and the Stalemate Machine." *Public Policy* 19 (1971): 217–274.

Evans, P. "Class, State, and Dependence in East Asia: Lessons for Latin Americanists." Pp. 203–226 in *The Political Economy of the New Asian Industrialism*, edited by F.C. Deyo. Ithaca, N.Y.: Cornell University Press, 1987.

Fei, J.C.H., G. Ranis, and S.W.Y. Kuo. *Growth With Equity: The Taiwan Case*. New York: Oxford University Press, 1979.

Friedman, D. *The Misunderstood Miracle: Industrial Development and Political Change in Japan*. Ithaca, N.Y.: Cornell University Press, 1988.

Gilpin, R. *U.S. Power and the Multinational Corporation*. New York: Basic Books, 1975.

Gold, T. B. *State and Society in the Taiwan Miracle*. Armonk, N.Y.: Sharpe, 1986.

Gourevitch, P. A. (ed.). *The Pacific Region: Challenges to Policy and Theory*. Newbury Park, Calif.: Sage, 1989.

Gurr, T. R. *Why Men Rebel*. Princeton, N.J.: Princeton University Press, 1970.

Haggard, S. "The Newly Industrializing Countries in the International System." *World Politics* 38 (1986): 343–370.

Haggard, S., and C. I. Moon. "The South Korean State in the International Economy: Liberal, Dependent, or Mercantile?" Pp. 131–190 in *The Antinomies of Interdependence*, edited by J. G. Ruggie. New York: Columbia University Press, 1983.

Harding, H. *China's Second Revolution: Reform After Mao*. Washington, D.C.: The Brookings Institution, 1987.

Hirschman, A. O. *National Power and the Structure of Foreign Trade*. Berkeley: University of California Press, 1945.

Hofheinz, R., Jr., and K. E. Calder. *The Eastasia Edge*. New York: Basic Books, 1982.

Huang, C. "The State and Foreign Investment: The Cases of Taiwan and Singapore." *Comparative Political Studies* 22 (1989): 93–121.

Johnson, C. *MITI and the Japanese Miracle*. Stanford, Calif.: Stanford University Press, 1982.

Jones, L., and I. Sakong. *Government, Business, and Entrepreneurship in Economic Development: The Korean Case.* Cambridge, Mass.: Harvard University Press, 1980.

Kahn, H. "The Confucian Ethic and Economic Growth." Pp. 78–80 in *The Gap Between the Rich and Poor,* edited by M. A. Seligson. Boulder, Colo.: Westview Press, 1984.

Keohane, R. O. *After Hegemony: Cooperation and Discord in the World Political Economy.* Princeton, N.J.: Princeton University Press, 1984.

Keohane, R. O., and J. S. Nye. *Power and Interdependence: World Politics in Transition.* Boston: Little, Brown, 1977.

Kim, S. (ed.). *China and the World: New Directions in Chinese Foreign Policy.* Boulder, Colo.: Westview Press, 1989.

Kindleberger, C. P. *The World in Depression, 1929–1939.* Berkeley: University of California Press, 1973.

Krasner, S. D. "State Power and the Structure of International Trade." *World Politics* 28 (1976): 317–347.

Kuznets, S. "Economic Growth and Income Inequality." *American Economic Review* 45 (1955): 1–28.

Lau, S. K. "Social Change, Bureaucratic Rule, and Emergent Political Issues in Hong Kong." *World Politics* 35 (1983): 544–563.

Levy, M. J., Jr. "Contrasting Factors in the Modernization of China and Japan." *Economic Development and Cultural Change* 2 (1953–54): 161–197.

Linder, S. B. *The Pacific Century: Economic and Political Consequences of Asian-Pacific Dynamism.* Stanford, Calif.: Stanford University Press, 1986.

Lipset, S. M. "Some Social Requisites of Democracy: Economic Development and Political Legitimacy." *American Political Science Review* 53 (1959): 69–105.

Mahler, V. A. *Dependency Approaches to International Political Economy: A Cross-National Study.* New York: Columbia University Press, 1980.

Merritt, R. *Symbols of American Community.* New Haven, Conn.: Yale University Press, 1966.

Miller, N. R. "Pluralism and Social Choice." *American Political Science Review* 77 (1983): 734–747.

Modelski, G. *Long Cycles in World Politics.* Seattle: University of Washington Press, 1987.

———— (ed.). *Exploring Long Cycles.* Boulder, Colo.: Lynne Rienner, 1987.

Moon, C. I. "Complex Interdependence and Transnational Lobbying: South Korea in the United States." *International Studies Quarterly* 32 (1988): 67–89.

Morawetz, D. *Why the Emperor's Clothes Are Not Made in Colombia?* London: Oxford University Press, 1981.

Moulder, F. V. *Japan, China and the Modern World Economy.* New York: Cambridge University Press, 1979.

Odell, J. S. "The Outcomes of International Trade Conflicts: The U.S. and South Korea, 1960–1981." *International Studies Quarterly* 29 (1985): 263–286.

Olson, M., Jr. *The Rise and Decline of Nations.* New Haven, Conn.: Yale University Press, 1982.

———. "Rapid Growth As A Destabilizing Force." *Journal of Economic History* 23 (1963): 529–552.

Olson, M., Jr., and R. Zeckhauser. "An Economic Theory of Alliances." *Review of Economics and Statistics* 48 (1966): 266–279.

Organski, A.F.K., and J. Kugler. *The War Ledger.* Chicago: University of Chicago Press, 1980.

Ozawa, T. *Multinationalism: Japanese Style.* Princeton, N.J.: Princeton University Press, 1979.

Pempel, T. J. "Japanese Foreign Economic Policy: The Domestic Bases for International Behavior." Pp. 139–190 in *Between Power and Plenty*, edited by P.J. Katzenstein. Madison: University of Wisconsin Press, 1978.

Pye, L. W. *China: An Introduction.* Boston: Little, Brown, 1984.

Rasler, K. A., and W. R. Thompson. "War-Making and State-Making: Governmental Expenditures, Tax Revenues, and Global War." *American Political Science Review* 79 (1985): 491–507.

Rosecrance, R. *The Rise of the Trading State: Commerce and Conquest in the Modern World.* New York: Basic Books, 1986.

Russett, B. M. "The Mysterious Case of Vanishing Hegemony; Or, Is Mark Twain Really Dead?" *International Organization* 39 (1985): 207–232.

———. "Defense Expenditures and National Well-Being." *American Political Science Review* 76 (1982): 767–777.

———. *What Price Vigilance? The Burdens of National Defense.* New Haven, Conn.: Yale University Press, 1970.

———. "Refining Deterrence Theory: The Japanese Attack on Pearl Harbor." Pp. 127–135 in *Theory and Research on the Causes of War*, edited by D. G. Pruitt and R. C. Snyder. Englewood Cliffs, N.J.: Prentice-Hall, 1969.

Samuels, R. J. "Consuming for Production: Japanese National Security, Nuclear Fuel Procurement, and the Domestic Economy." *International Organization* 43 (1989): 625–646.

Schmiegelow, M. "Cutting Across Doctrines: Positive Adjustment in Japan." *International Organization* 39 (1985): 261–296.

Simon, S. W. "The ASEAN States: Obstacles to Security Cooperation." *ORBIS* 22 (1978): 415–434.

Singer, J. D., S. Bremer, and J. Stuckey. "Capability Distribution, Uncertainty, and Major Power War, 1820–1965." Pp. 19–48 in *Peace, War, and Numbers*, edited by B. M. Russett. Beverly Hills, Calif.: Sage, 1972.

Snidal, D. "The Limits of Hegemonic Stability Theory." *International Organization* 37 (1985): 579–614.

Starr, H. "A Collective Goods Analysis of Warsaw Pact After Czechoslovakia." *International Organization* 28 (1974): 521–532.

Stein, A. A. "The Hegemon's Dilemmas: Great Britain, the United States, and the International Economic Order." *International Organization* 38 (1984): 355–386.

Strange, S. "The Persistent Myth of Lost Hegemony." *International Organization* 41 (1987): 551–574.

Tow, W. T., and W. R. Feeney (eds.). *U.S. Foreign Policy and Asia-Pacific Security.* Boulder, Colo.: Westview Press, 1982.

Vogel, E. F. *Japan As Number 1.* New York: Harper & Row, 1979.

Wallerstein, I. *The Modern World-System: Capitalist Agriculture and the Origins of the European World-Economy in the Sixteenth Century.* New York: Academic Press, 1974.

Weber, M. *The Religion of China.* New York: Macmillan, 1964.

Whiting, A. S. *Siberian Development and East Asia: Threat or Promise?* Stanford, Calif.: Stanford University Press, 1981.

Winckler, E. A., and S. Greenhalgh (eds.). *Contending Approaches to the Political Economy of Taiwan.* Armonk, N.Y.: Sharpe, 1988.

Yoffie, D. B. *Power and Protectionism: Strategies of the Newly Industrializing Countries.* New York: Columbia University Press, 1983.

Zagoria, D. *The Vietnam Triangle.* New York: Pegasus, 1967.

□ □ □

Glossary

Balance-of-power theory argues that international peace is more likely to be maintained when there is a rough balance of capabilities between two or more rival countries or alliances than when one country or alliance has a preponderance of capabilities.

Command economy is one in which the government allocates economic resources, stipulates production targets, and sets prices according to a master plan.

Comparative advantage is a particular economic asset (e.g., abundant resources, advanced technology, cheap labor) that enables a company or country to produce a good more efficiently than others can.

Complex interdependence characterizes international relations in which military power becomes less usable, nonsecurity issues gain increasing salience, multiple domestic and foreign actors enter the policy arena, the distinction between domestic and foreign policies is blurred, and the issue agenda and status hierarchy in foreign relations are fluid and changeable.

Composition of trade is the content of a country's trade portfolio, such as the relative shares of agricultural, mineral, manufactured, and industrial goods in its exports.

Comprehensive national security refers to the Japanese idea of combining military security with economic and political security by developing friendly political ties with important neighbors, assuring continued access to foreign markets, and searching for safe investment opportunities and stable resource supplies abroad.

Containment policy was the name of the U.S. policy of erecting political and military alliances in the 1950s and 1960s in order to prevent the spread of communism.

Dependency theory argues that Third World countries are highly dependent on the capital, technology, and markets of the developed countries, that this dependence results in the exploitation and domination of Third World countries by developed countries, and that this exploitation and domination have in turn been responsible for the underdevelopment of Third World countries.

Developmental state is a government that intervenes actively in the economy in order to guide or promote particular substantive goals (e.g., full employment, export competitiveness, energy self-sufficiency).

Distributional coalitions are interest groups (labor unions, professional associations, producer cartels) that try to gain particular financial or social advantages for their members (usually at the expense of the economic productivity of society as a whole).

Electoral cycling refers to the tendency for officials with different political persuasions and policy inclinations to alternate the control of government as a result of changing electoral outcomes.

Export expansion is an outward-looking strategy that emphasizes foreign trade as a way of promoting domestic economic growth.

Free rider is a country (or person) that tries to benefit from a public good that it has not adequately paid for.

Hegemonic stability theory argues that only the leading global power has the means and the will to provide international order and stability.

Import substitution is an inward-looking strategy that emphasizes the development of domestic industries in order to achieve self-sufficiency in certain areas (e.g., consumer durables, intermediate goods).

Laissez-faire economy is characterized by the classical (or neoclassical) economic doctrine that contends that governments should refrain from interfering with the market.

Lateral pressure describes the tendency toward foreign expansion and international rivalry that occurs when countries experience rapid economic and population growth.

Long cycles are regular periods of about one century that have coincided with the rise and decline of global leadership of a dominant power in the past 500 years.

Orderly marketing agreement is a bilateral arrangement to restrict the quantity of certain imports.

Phoenix factor refers to the tendency for the countries defeated in a war to achieve faster economic growth in the postwar period than the victorious countries.

Power transition theory argues that international war is more likely to happen when one country catches up with and overtakes another country than when one country has a preponderance of power.

Public good is a benefit (international peace, stability, order) that has the characteristics of nondivisibility and nonexcludabilty.

Regimes consist of norms, rules, principles, and shared expectations that provide a basis for institutions and conventions to deal with international conduct.

Regional bigemony is the rule of two hegemons.

Regulatory state characterizes a government that refrains from interfering in the marketplace, except to ensure certain limited procedural goals (e.g., antitrust regulations, protection of consumer rights).

Relative deprivation is a sense of frustration stemming from a perceived gap between one's current position in life and one's aspirations or expectations.

Scarcity rent refers to the profits accrued by producers when a shortage of supply drives up the price of goods.

Security community is a region in which people settle their disputes without resort to war or the threat of war.

Statist theory argues that governments of the late-industrializing countries must play an active and leading role in their economic development.

Structural power is the ability to determine the rules of international relations; it reflects superior capabilities in military force, economic productivity, monetary and financial assets, and knowledge development and accumulation.

Terms of trade means the balance of payments in foreign trade; it can be favorable or unfavorable depending on whether the value of one's exports exceeds that of imports or vice versa.

Voluntary export restraint is a bilateral agreement to restrict the quantity of certain imports.

World system refers to the structure of international relations among the capitalist countries; it is primarily based on a division of labor whereby some countries specialize in the production of primary goods and others specialize in the manufacture of industrial goods.

□ □ □

Index

□ □ □

About the Book and Author

Will the rise of the Pacific Basin in the world economy be matched by changes in political order and a strengthening of regional security? Can the superpowers come to grips with a challenger wielding economic clout rather than weaponry?

East Asian Dynamism is a succinct account of the political economy of the Pacific region from the dawn of the modern world system through projections of alternative future scenarios. It applies theoretical perspectives from history, sociology, economics, and political science to countries and events selected both for their analytical power and their substantive importance.

While exploring the cardinal values of growth, order, and security, Steve Chan takes us inside Japan Inc. and the Four Little Tigers, evaluates the effects of China's modernization, and then expands his analysis to embrace Soviet Siberia and Western North America. Introducing us to a region whose geography, history, and culture are often regarded as mysteries, Professor Chan brings to life the current policy choices and dilemmas facing the people and leaders of this region. In the process, he answers questions about what constitutes economic success, whether there are alternatives to the U.S. regional "security blanket," and what the policy competition, tradeoffs, and cross-currents are from domestic and foreign perspectives.

Replete with examples, case studies, and cutting-edge concepts, *East Asian Dynamism* is ideal for students of international relations, security studies, international political economy, foreign policy, and Asian studies. Maps, tables of descriptive data, suggested readings, and a glossary are featured additions to the basic text.

Steve Chan is professor of political science at the University of Colorado–Boulder. He has written numerous books and articles on East Asian and international political economy and is the author of a leading international relations textbook.